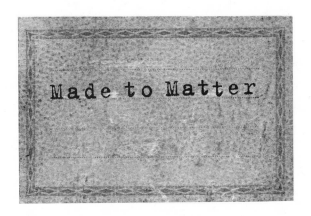

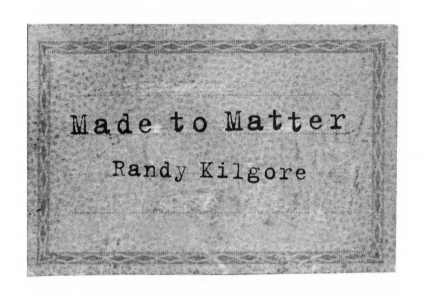

Made to Matter

Randy Kilgore

DEVOTIONS FOR
WORKING CHRISTIANS

DISCOVERY HOUSE

PUBLISHERS®

Feeding the Soul with the Word of God

Discovery House Publishers is affiliated with RBC Ministries,
Grand Rapids, Michigan.

Discovery House books are distributed to the trade exclusively by
Barbour Publishing, Inc., Uhrichsville, Ohio.

Requests for permission to quote from this book should be directed to:
Permissions Department, Discovery House Publishers, P.O. Box 3566,
Grand Rapids, MI 49501.

Unless otherwise indicated, Scripture taken from the *New American Standard
Bible,* © Copyright 1960, 1962, 1963, 1968, 1971, 1972, 1973, 1975, 1977, 1995
by the Lockman Foundation. Used by permission.

Interior design by Sherri Hoffman

Library of Congress Cataloging-in-Publication Data

Kilgore, Randy.
 Made to matter : devotions for applying faith in the workplace / Randy
Kilgore.
    p. cm.
  ISBN 978-1-57293-267-8
  1. Employees--Prayers and devotions. 2. Work--Prayers and devotions. 3.
Work--Religious aspects--Christianity--Meditations. I. Title.
  BV4593.K55 2008
  242'.68--dc22

                       2008030757

Printed in the United States of America
08 09 10 11 12/ SB /10 9 8 7 6 5 4 3 2 1

Dedication

For Refa and Ernie Kilgore

Contents

Acknowledgments   9

Introduction: Made to Matter   11

Week 1: From a Dusty Tent in Egypt   13

Week 2: God's Timeless Gift to Workers   17

Week 3: He Also Made Me Fast!   21

Week 4: I Only Want to Matter   23

Week 5: I Have Come to Help   27

Week 6: A Faith with Muscle   29

Week 7: Ten-Minute Christians   31

Week 8: Return to Honor   35

Week 9: Keeper of the Lights   37

Week 10: If Jesus Came Today   41

Week 11: Workplace Legacies   43

Week 12: The Reason We Exist   45

Week 13: One Soul at a Time   47

Week 14: You Feed Them   49

Week 15: Ethan's Story   51

Week 16: Legacies   53

Week 17: It's That Moment   55

Week 18: Still Standing   57

Week 19: Courage, Character, and Civility   59

Week 20: Talking about God at Work   63

Week 21: Sometimes, Rest   65

Week 22: Making a Difference at Work   67

Week 23: A Leader Like That   69

Week 24: Hard to Lead from the Rear   71

Week 25: It Ought to Be Easier   73

Week 26: Compensation 77

Week 27: A Work/Faith Journey, Part 1 79

Week 28: A Work/Faith Journey, Part 2 83

Week 29: More Than We Can Bear 85

Week 30: Red Sox Missionaries in a Yankees World 87

Week 31: Prayers for the Workplace 89

Week 32: Why Do You Work? 91

Week 33: The Damage of a Hectic Pace 93

Week 34: Separation Canyon 95

Week 35: Nothing But Net 97

Week 36: The Only Port That Matters 99

Week 37: Best Practices 101

Week 38: Points to Ponder 105

Week 39: The Source of Our Significance 107

Week 40: Bring On the Storms 109

Week 41: Unemployment's Spiritual Challenges 111

Week 42: The Other Side of Why 113

Week 43: Let Me See the Chariots 115

Week 44: One More Year 117

Week 45: The Lord's Commission 119

Week 46: The Best Argument 121

Week 47: Eyes on the Fence Post 123

Week 48: Your God Matters at Work 125

Week 49: The End of Empty Nets 127

Week 50: He's Already There 129

Week 51: Who Is My Neighbor? 131

Week 52: The Last Christmas Tale 133

Week 53: Old Ideas for a New Year 137

Acknowledgments

WRITING IS OFTEN THE ART of slowing down and noticing things other people miss, or it's having the freedom to say what other people are too busy to stop and record. Good writing moves from self-reflection to observation and from observation to service. No writer makes that journey alone. Certainly I haven't.

I owe the most to my wife, of course. For thirty-plus years she's been the one steady influence that never changed. Even the worst of life's storms didn't shake her. She's the first in a long line of powerful influences. Next in line are Francis and Norma Allen, who introduced me to faith and then made sure I knew how to keep growing. Years later, Milton May moved from college advisor to lifelong mentor. While Francis and Norma set the course, it was Milton who made the course corrections that helped me learn to use my gifts. Constant in the journey was my father, a truck driver who always found ways to express his love and support.

The list goes on and on, of course. Every worker I ever met is part of something you find here—every friend and family member, too.

Annette Selden found my writing and convinced Discovery House to explore it, then moved alongside me as editor when the project was approved. She's been a master at nudging me to phrases that make the text stronger, and her spiritual depth has always been apparent in her coaching.

Last, but certainly not least, of course, are Ethan and Kathryn. I'm convinced that all the secrets of life were locked up inside me until I became a dad. Every day is a treasure hunt now.

INTRODUCTION

Made to Matter

THE WORDS OF ROBERT FROST'S "The Road Not Taken" echo through our souls, leaving us to wonder if we've missed, somehow, the path God really wanted us to take. This is especially true when we find ourselves tangled in the briars of our present path.

Did we miss the chance to matter? Is there something we should have done to make life more exciting, more productive, more meaningful? Is it too late to change?

This is not a struggle unique to Christians. Nearly all the people I've met over the past thirty years—first when I worked as a human resource manager and now a workplace chaplain—describe a moment when they found themselves wondering if they shouldn't have turned left when the path jutted right.

For many, the angst of the "what-ifs" and "almosts" merely whets an appetite for nostalgia, a harkening back to times when we thought there were still choices to be made and life to be lived with youthful zest. For some, those "what-ifs" leave an ache that fuels thoughts best given voice by Thoreau when he suggested most of us "lead lives of quiet desperation."

For Christians, often these nagging questions vault to a spiritual crisis. Indoctrinated as so many of us are in the myth that God has only one perfect design for us—and reminded constantly of our inability to be perfect—we can't help but wonder if our trains didn't jump the tracks long ago.

So we read the tales of missionaries from the past and sit in our pews admiring pastors for their commitment to God and convince ourselves we're somehow second-class citizens in the kingdom of God.

Nothing could be further from the truth!

We were made to matter, and the majesty of God is not just that He created us to live lives that make important contributions but that He continues to provide us—daily—with ways to matter in the places where we find ourselves this moment.

Even more glorious is the discovery that for His children, those who recognize their need for Jesus Christ, there is always redemption as God continues to pick us up even after wrong choices have carried us miles down the path of fruitless living.

He even records it in His Word, this factoid of faithful shepherding: "For a righteous man falls seven times, and rises again," Proverbs 24:16 teaches us.

So it is with this life, where an infinitely patient Father picks His own back up and finds new ways for them to matter right where their journeys have carried them. In the pages that follow, we seek to remind each other and ourselves just how often the real world we live in is made whole by the words of the God who created it. Each devotional wrestles with a moment nearly everyone faces and guides us back to the truth that God made us to matter: to Him, to each other, and to this place where we live and work day in and day out.

Then, when even our best efforts to pick ourselves up falter or when we're too tired to take one more step or we're too weak or sick to work, God reminds us of an even deeper truth: that the reason we exist is to be in relationship with Him. So even in those moments when actions are impossible, we haven't lost our worth.

We matter because He made us; we matter because He made us to live and work in community with others; and we matter because He made us to mirror Him every moment of every day in every place. May you draw strength, comfort, inspiration, joy, purpose, and even humor as we travel as co-laborers down the paths we've chosen.

WEEK 1

From a Dusty Tent in Egypt

Oh give thanks to the LORD, for He is good, for His lovingkindness is everlasting. Let the redeemed of the LORD say so, whom He has redeemed from the hand of the adversary (PSALM 107:1–2).

WHO COULD IMAGINE THE MOUNTAINS God was building in a dusty tent in that 1915 desert?

Zeitoun, Egypt, was a staging area for Allied soldiers heading to Gallipoli and other fronts of the War to End All Wars, as World War One was known at the time. In a world gone mad, fewer than half the soldiers who passed through the dusty tents of Zeitoun would live to see their homes again.

At each staging area, the Young Men's Christian Association (YMCA) organized services for the soldiers away from home. While other leaders of the YMCA entertained troops with concerts and the new invention, moving pictures, Oswald, the secretary in charge at Zeitoun, opted instead for Bible classes. His peers chuckled at his innocence. Some likely thought him daft.

But Oswald knew something they didn't: *People want to listen when they think they may hear God.* So Oswald offered these world-weary, duty-driven, war-ravaged soldiers something called biblical psychology, and a strange thing happened: He packed the house!

Imagine the picture. Hundreds of burly soldiers crowded into a tent studying something called biblical psychology. Not on Sundays only. Not occasionally. Not once a week. *Every night!*

Early on in that First World War, earnest Christian leaders desperately sought to explain God to a world reeling beneath the weight of "man's inhumanity to man." The world didn't seem to hear them. Frustrated by this rebuff and beleaguered by their own doubts, many followers of Jesus slipped into puzzled silence.

Not Oswald. *"I don't care what God does,"* he once told his wife, *"I care who God is."*

How could this apparently callous comment bring comfort to anyone?

But Oswald understood human nature better than his peers. He knew men and women who could make sense of little else were hungry to know there was more to life than the hours that lay ahead of them. He knew they wanted more than mere distraction. They wanted answers that were bigger than the moment at hand, answers bigger than the circumstances. *Answers he possessed because of his intimate relationship with the Almighty!*

How callous not to share them; how senseless to merely distract or entertain these soldiers when eternity was so close to reality for so many of them.

So Oswald stopped trying to explain the unexplainable, stopped trying to answer the unanswerable, and focused instead on the story he knew: *who God is.*

Did he have an impact? Thousands of soldiers passed through the tents of Zeitoun en route to final resting places on battlefields far from home. History tells us hundreds, probably even thousands, passed from those fields to the presence of God, saved by grace only days before in the dusty tents of Zeitoun.

Did he have an impact? Two years later, when the young chaplain died suddenly of complications from appendicitis, the soldiers he served insisted, mind you, *pleaded,* for the right to bury him with full military honors. And so he was. Casket resting on gun carriage, officers in dress uniforms striding alongside. Rifles turned backwards in salute accompanied by the haunting lilt of a lonely bugle. Soldiers saying farewell in the only way they knew how to the man who spent his final hours teaching them "who God is."

Did he have an impact? You be the judge. When Oswald died, it seemed likely his words and work would die with him—that is, until Biddy (his wife) decided to collect them to distribute. A trained stenographer, for years she had been recording verbatim the words of her husband, Oswald, as he taught soldiers in Egypt and Bible students in other places.

After he died it was Biddy who put together one of the best-selling devotional books in human history: *My Utmost for His Highest* by Oswald Chambers, the chaplain in those tents of Egypt.

Who could have imagined the mountains God was building in a dusty tent in that 1915 desert?

You and I are surrounded every day by people weary of their journey, desperate for a word of hope in the midst of trial. They sometimes hide their fears behind angry words or silent stares or self-indulgent distractions aimed at anesthetizing their uncertainty. They sometimes even assault the very notion of God while privately pleading with Him to deliver a sign that makes them believe. They push and shove and shout at His ambassadors in hurtful and hateful ways while secretly hoping they find just one person who shows them something they can grasp to make them believers, too.

Not all, to be sure. God tells us with great sadness the road is full of people choosing to run away from Him. But shoulder to shoulder in our workplaces and churches and schools and homes is an army of people who are not running, people who are secretly longing to hear someone really teach them "who God is."

Let that person be you. Let that person be me. Who can imagine the mountains of hope God might be building in the dusty tents of our daily lives?

In the words of the psalmist, "Let the redeemed of the LORD say so."

WEEK 2

God's Timeless Gift to Workers

Then the LORD said to Moses, "See, I have chosen Bezalel son of Uri, the son of Hur, of the tribe of Judah, and I have filled him with the Spirit of God, with skill, ability and knowledge in all kinds of crafts—to make artistic designs for work in gold, silver and bronze, to cut and set stones, to work in wood, and to engage in all kinds of craftsmanship. Moreover, I have appointed Oholiab son of Ahisamach, of the tribe of Dan, to help him. Also I have given skill to all the craftsmen to make everything I have commanded you (EXODUS 31:1–6 NIV).*

UTTERLY ALONE, AT THE BOTTOM of a fourteen-foot trench filled with water so thick with silt he *literally* couldn't see his hand in front of his face, William Walker laid twenty-five thousand bags of concrete, slitting each bag open so the concrete could spread out as it set. He then used 115,000 concrete blocks and 900,000 bricks to shore up the national treasure we know as Winchester Cathedral.

Every morning, five mornings a week, fifty weeks a year, for six years and one month, from 1905 to 1911, Walker would climb into his diver's suit and wait while his tenders loaded forty-pound stones over his shoulders and placed a fifty-pound metal helmet over his head. Then he would step into eighteen-pound metal shoes and descend into the depths of the trench around Winchester Cathedral to work for three-and-a-half hours.

After an hour for lunch, he would go through the ritual again in order to work another three-and-a-half hours in the pitch dark completely alone.

Incredibly, the majestic structure that thrills people even today with its remarkable architecture had been built on a bog, floating on what Sir

Francis Fox called a "raft" of massive beech timbers. As the timbers rotted, the mighty building started to sag.

It isn't stretching things at all to say William Walker single-handedly saved Winchester Cathedral.

Since the water swirled in and out of sites where bubonic plague victims had been buried centuries earlier, Walker also had to worry about exposure to life-threatening infectious materials and the possibility of encountering floating skeletal remains. His response: "I try not to think too much about that."

So day in and day out, week in and week out, year in and year out, Walker fought to save a structure built by long-dead humans to honor a still-living God.

What a magnificent story!

In a perfect world where happy endings always happen, William Walker would have lived a long life bathed in the adoration of the English people for his unseen labors. In a perfect world, a famous sculptor would craft a statue to sit in the halls of the Cathedral to honor Walker's name. In a perfect world, visitors to the tombs of William the Conqueror and Jane Austen would see and remember the face of the man who saved an irreplaceable part of England's history.

Alas, to use the king's own English, *'tis not a perfect world we rest in.*

William Walker would be one of the millions and millions of people felled by the flu pandemic that swept the world in 1918. When the sculptor sat down to craft the monument to Walker, *he used a photo of the wrong man*, and the Church of England, embarrassed by its error, refused to correct it for almost ninety years.

But William Walker knew something most of us need to learn or, having once learned it, need to be reminded of again and again and again.

It isn't adoration or statues or even the satisfaction of a job well done that is God's gift to His children.

It's the work itself!

Hard as it is to imagine, even those things we do in the places nobody can see, even when we're weighed down by heavy trials, even when we don't have the joy of the company of coworkers, the labor we're engaged in is God's gift to us.

Let the coal miner rejoice. Let the bond trader exult. Let firefighters and architects and school teachers glory in their labor, for God in His infinite wisdom has given them the chance to play a role in shoring up the foundations of a creation built to last forever.

One day, when every knee has bowed and every tongue confessed that Jesus Christ is Lord, every dark hour, every tedious task, every ounce of effort given by God's children to the tending of His cathedral will see the light of day, and we will know and count it as great treasure that God let us be a small part of His big work.

WEEK 3

He Also Made Me Fast!

Whatever you do, do your work heartily, as for the Lord rather than for men (COLOSSIANS 3:23).

So will My word be which goes forth from My mouth; it will not return to Me empty, without accomplishing what I desire, and without succeeding in the matter for which I sent it (ISAIAH 55:11).

"I believe God made me for a purpose—for China. But He also made me fast! And when I run, I feel His pleasure. To give that up would be to hold Him in contempt."
—ERIC LIDDELL in film dialogue from *Chariots of Fire*

ERIC LIDDELL NEVER SAW WINNING the Olympic medal as the purpose of his life. His purpose, his life service, would be the work he did as a missionary, ultimately becoming a martyr for the cause of Christ in China. But he understood what many of us in the workplace struggle to understand or recall: honoring God is about doing our best in today's work, not waiting for tomorrow's promise. Being competent in the place God has us *right now* is how we honor Him. Whatever we're doing this day—driving a truck, managing a company, plowing a field, punching a keyboard, tending children—*now* is the moment God calls us to honor Him.

If a first key step in shaping our workplace is forming a bond with other believers, then the second must surely be competence in the task before us this day. Developing ourselves into effective and valued workers is a vital building block for influencing our work culture. God may indeed choose to use someone who is not competent to bring glory to Himself, but more often the most effective impact for Christ comes when we do our work responsibly and competently, honoring the time and resources of our employer. We often fail in our efforts to honor God because we fail in honoring our employers.

Employers, coworkers, and customers who trust our *daily* efforts are more likely to trust our *spiritual* efforts also.

Just as we must be competent in the job, *we must also be competent in our handling of the Scriptures on the job*. It is essential we find ways to steep ourselves in the truths of the Bible. Life at work seldom allows time to stop and find a passage of Scripture that applies to the task before us. Rather we must work to commit the truths of the Bible to our minds so they are accessible in the heat of workplace moments. Even in the most boring of our quiet times, God is at work making His Word come alive in us, as our Scripture passage notes.

We see in these passages that as we read His Word He begins to work, revealing truth to us. He is also faithful to bring those truths forward as we go about the routine tasks of life. *His Word will not return empty!* Now our decisions at work can be guided by those truths, and our culture begins to be influenced by them through us.

Eric Liddell won the gold medal in the Olympics and then slipped into the tiny villages of China to serve Christ there. *"He made me fast!"* was but one scene among many in his life. He didn't wait to reach China to serve God but served Him in the circumstance—and with the skills—God gave Him each moment.

"He also made me _____!"

How we complete that sentence defines where we serve Him next. Tomorrow is not the time to be competent. We must do it now.

WEEK 4

I Only Want to Matter

And [Jesus] said to him, " 'You shall love the LORD *your God with all your heart, and with all your soul, and with all your mind.' This is the great and foremost commandment. The second is like it, 'You shall love your neighbor as yourself' "* (MATTHEW 22:37–39).

A DRIVING RAIN PELTED ME as I ran to the front of the building, only to hear that maddening clatter you get when you pull on locked glass doors. Mercifully, an elderly woman moved toward the doors from inside and in short order had me comfortably settled in the lobby. Like an elegant hostess, she sat with me there—dust rag in hand—and chatted as I waited for a senior manager in the firm to show up for our meeting.

"I clean this office," she said in what I later learned was an East European accent, moving her arm in a sweeping motion to show me the lobby. "What do you do?" I told her a little about my work as a Christian writer (which puzzled and bored her, I think), but when I mentioned I was also a chaplain, she perked right up. "I, too, am a Christian." She said it with a certainty and a satisfaction that must surely have pleased God. I waited for her to tell me more, but only silence followed.

"Am I keeping you from your work?" I asked, not wanting to get her in trouble. She shook her head to indicate I wasn't and then explained that she always finished early and added, "I like to come down here and watch the people come to work." There was a hint of loneliness to this last statement, an almost wistful whisper of sadness. So I asked her more questions about her story.

At first her answers were brief. It was obvious she was used to short attention spans, people asking questions to be polite but with little interest in the answers. When she realized I was interested, though, she settled into the role of storyteller with delight. I was treated to delicious tidbits of her personal history that had us both smiling.

All the people who were important to her were no longer around. I wasn't made privy to the details of their absence, and my hostess-turned-storyteller had too much dignity to complain. Whether they died or moved away or simply neglected her wasn't part of the tale I had permission to know. Only once, when she was telling me a part of someone else's woes, did I get a glimpse of her own thoughts. Describing that person's loneliness, she said quietly, "They only want to matter to someone."

It's a phrase I hear repeated about as often in my work as any other, though people seldom say it directly. In a work world that values efficiency and action; that places great emphasis on busyness and productivity; that wrestles to squeeze the most out of every action; one of the byproducts is often loneliness. It's a disease as prevalent in the senior reaches of a firm as it is in the bowels of the operation. It stretches outside the workplace to our families, leaving children feeling this same gnawing emptiness that haunts adults. Always, the sentiment emerges: "I only want to matter to someone."

For most people I meet, telling them they matter to God is not enough. God seems distant and surreal to people who have little or no tangible connections to other human beings. But the reality of a loving God literally leaps out to those whose loneliness and isolation is ended by mattering to someone here on earth.

It struck me as I listened to my hostess on that early gray morning that one of the most important ways workplace Christians can serve God is by caring about the people they work with every day, especially those who usually fall below our radar screens.

Among the many majestic things about Jesus during His time on earth was His wonderful ability to notice the lonely and to reach out to them in warm and intimate ways. "Zaccheus," Jesus said, "I *must* stay at your house today." How important that must have made Zaccheus feel! How easy it is for us to love others simply by taking note of them. If we truly wish to honor God at work today, then we do that best by honoring those He created who work in the next cubicle or the next office, whether they're wielding dust rags or the power to hire and fire us.

When my friend, the senior manager, arrived for our appointment, he greeted my hostess by name and thanked her for taking care of me while I waited. She nodded shyly and smiled, then looked at me and answered, "I didn't want him to be lonely in this big place."

I wasn't.

WEEK 5

I Have Come to Help

But prove yourselves doers of the word, and not merely hearers who delude themselves (JAMES 1:22).

NEW YORK CITY REPORTER JACOB Riis made it his business to let the world know what being poor was like. His vivid descriptions of ghetto life in nineteenth-century New York horrified a generally complacent public. His "magic lantern show" of photographs taken of the poor in New York so stunned lecture halls that his audiences felt they were present in the tenements themselves. Many fainted, and it is said not a few talked aloud to the people in the photos.

Riis's book, *How the Other Half Lives*, combined his writing with his own photographs to paint a picture so vivid the public could not escape the certainty of its existence. The third of fifteen children born to Danish parents, Riis wrote so effectively because, once upon a time, he lived in that world of terrible despair after his arrival in the United States at the age of twenty-one.

Shortly after the release of his book, a card was delivered to Riis from a young man only then beginning his political career. The card read simply, *"I have read your book, and I have come to help. Theodore Roosevelt."*

Hard-nosed, skeptical, world-weary Riis immediately became a disciple of the future president for life.

It is not enough for us to pull ourselves up by our bootstraps, to successfully conquer obstacles and become self-sufficient. Our individual lives must be trailblazing, leaving not scorched earth but well-lit paths that others may follow out of the same perilous plights we once faced. Like Jacob

Riis, once an impoverished immigrant determined to make a difference, we owe it to the tired and poor to call attention to their plight and not merely celebrate the fact that we made it out of that morass ourselves. We owe it to our God to love others so much that the memories of their poverty wrest us from our complacency to a place of action.

Those who have never known the ache of need are called to write with our lives and resources "cards" that read like Roosevelt's note: *"I have seen your need, and I have come to help."* Not only to write, but to act. (*"Be doers and not hearers only."*) Hope in the midst of despair often comes merely by hearing that others are coming.

....

Followers of Jesus Christ know both sides of this equation. Confronted by the squalor of sin in their lives, no hope existed for rescue from the darkness of present and eternal separation from a loving God. No amount of good deeds could bridge the gap or quench the darkness of the soul.

Then God read the book of our lives.

In a bed made of straw that was surrounded by a stunned young couple, shepherds still covered with the dust of their journey, and a world desperately in need of some sign of hope, a tiny baby's birth echoed these words: "I have come to help."

WEEK 6

A Faith with Muscle

I have been crucified with Christ; and it is no longer I who live, but Christ lives in me; and the life which I now live in the flesh I live by faith in the Son of God, who loved me and gave Himself up for me (GALATIANS 2:20).

WE CANNOT TEACH WHAT WE do not know, but we also cannot truly know what we do not teach.

....

Dwight L. Moody's thunderous voice boomed the gospel to the mighty and the meek in 1885 London. Grimy dockworkers mixed with the privileged, all eager to hear this upstart American roar about a faith that changes lives.

On this particular night, Moody had onstage with him the Cambridge Seven, army officers and athletes prominent in England. These were England's heroes, and they were there to declare their lives were surrendered to God for action in His kingdom. One of the seven challenged the audience to "proclaim themselves for Christ" by standing up. Slowly, one young lad in a naval uniform got the courage to stand, even though the shipmates with him needled him mercilessly.

Nobody remembers the name of the boy who stood, but sitting in the crowd watching all this was another young man named Wilfred Grenfell. Grenfell was already a Christian, soon to finish his medical training, but he lacked a sense that his faith made any difference in life—his or anyone else's. This night, though, mesmerized by the booming Moody, delighted at the heroes surrounding Moody on the stage, and moved by the courageous act of the boy/sailor, Grenfell stood up too. Later he would write, "I knew that the right way to use muscles was to use them, and I argued that a similar treatment is what faith needed."

Today, Grenfell is famous for taking the gospel—and medicine—to the hard shores of Labrador, into the bleak lives of the crews of the fishing fleets and their families. His ministry carved out a place for people to be cared for physically and opened the doors to their spiritual tending as well. Hospitals, hospital ships, clinics, and a healthy dose of the gospel brought light into the darkness, and physical and spiritual progress were all the result of the actions of an unknown sailor, a raucous preacher, and a bunch of heroes.

We cannot teach what we do not know. We often talk about the importance of the spiritual disciplines, of knowing God by knowing His Word. Quiet hours with God spent in Bible study and prayer slip silently out of our schedule in the midst of lives devoted to "doing" with no central theme, ships sailing out to war without rudders, armament, or missions. It is simply impossible for us to be ambassadors for Christ when we know little of His teaching and nothing of His direction for us. But it's equally true we cannot know what we do not teach. Ours is a faith with muscle, a faith able to root out even the darkest soul and restore it to God. To confine that faith to the walls of our homes or the walls of our churches is to forget the very things we read there, hear there, and learn there in the pages of God's Word. Our quiet hours with God are not meant to separate our faith from the rest of our lives but rather to launch it into those hours when all of humanity surrounds us, waiting for a Christian with purpose, with direction, with truth.

God intends that person to be you—and me. Get into your prayer closets, get into your Bible, but then get back out to your jobs and your world. Get out with vigor and a truth that gives rudders to your vessel and hope to a world spinning out of control.

WEEK 7

Ten-Minute Christians

[Jesus said,] "You are the salt of the earth; but if the salt has become tasteless, how can it be made salty again? It is no longer good for anything, except to be thrown out and trampled under foot by men. You are the light of the world. A city set on a hill cannot be hidden; nor does anyone light a lamp and put it under a basket, but on the lampstand, and it gives light to all who are in the house. Let your light shine before men in such a way that they may see your good works, and glorify your Father who is in heaven" (MATTHEW 5:13–16).

OLD SOLDIERS STILL CRY AT the mention of this story.

....

December 17, 1941. Citizens in North Platte, Nebraska, heard a rumor a troop train carrying their sons and daughters to war would be stopping at the local depot for ten minutes. They made plans to meet it and load the soldiers up with food, gifts, and magazines for the long, lonely train ride to an uncertain future. They knew some of those soldiers would never see home again.

Well, the train arrived all right, but not with *Nebraska* soldiers. They were *Kansans!*

(Cue awkward moment; townspeople standing around quietly with food baskets in hand; soldiers peeking out the windows wondering what's happening.) One person must have started forward, because suddenly these Nebraska farmers were greeting Kansas soldiers like they were their own.

Eight days later, on Christmas day, North Platte citizens started meeting every troop train—*every troop train*—from 5:00 a.m. until well after midnight, feeding lonely soldiers heading to places like Iwo Jima, Bastogne, Normandy, and Wake Island. In a time when everything was rationed, people from all over Nebraska and even parts of Colorado traded in their ration stamps for eggs and sugar and other staples so they could feed these traveling troops for ten minutes each. They did it without ever missing a train from December 25, 1941, to the last train served on April 1, 1946, serving six million—read that again, *six million*—soldiers in the process. Their hospitality carried the name of the North Platte Canteen to every corner of the world, making it probably the most talked-about town in the history of the American soldier.

Even the most battle-tested, life-hardened, crusty old troopers weep when they talk about what those ten minutes meant to them—what those moments *still* mean to them.

Especially in today's world, life is defined more by ten-minute encounters than ever before. The customer across the counter, the worker chatting by the water cooler, the vendor stopping in to stock the shelf, the driver in the car that just cut us off on our commute.

What do people remember when they walk away from these ten-minute encounters with us? How do we prepare our hearts to touch the lives of people who pass by us so fast that the residue of our meeting only hits them when they're gone? What work will we do before they arrive that make those ten minutes useful or, in rare instances, even memorable?

This is an era for ten-minute Christians, where opportunities to serve slip past us so quickly we can come to see them as meaningless. Eye contact, warm words, kind words, and going the extra mile aren't just good business; they're good witnesses, too.

To a world trapped on trains to the wrong side of eternity, a stopover with a follower of Jesus Christ might be just the seed the Holy Spirit uses to bring them to the kingdom. The weary, discouraged, and overwhelmed—believer and nonbeliever—need a ten-minute stopover in an oasis of faith. Even the strong among us find strength for the journey when we encounter Jesus reflected in surprising places and surprising faces. Citizens in North Platte knew something we need to learn: Ten minutes can change a life.

Six million soldiers headed away from North Platte with a nugget of home and hope tucked safely in their hearts. May the people who meet us this day get a glimpse of the hope we have tucked in our hearts.

WEEK 8

Return to Honor

Suffer hardship with me, as a good soldier of Christ Jesus
(2 TIMOTHY 2:3).

[TWENTY-ONE STEPS. TURN TO FACE the tomb and pause for twenty-one seconds. Twenty-one steps in the opposite direction. Turn to face the tomb and pause for twenty-one seconds. Twenty-one steps in the opposite direction . . . Twenty-four hours a day. Three hundred sixty-five days a year. Rain, sleet, hail, thunder, lightning.]

In September 2003, a terrible storm bore down on Washington, DC. For the first time in the history of the Tomb of the Unknowns, soldiers guarding the burial site of these honored dead at Arlington National Cemetery were given permission to leave their posts for safety if Hurricane Isabel came. The guards' response?

Not a chance!

So through driving rain and havoc-wreaking winds, while the city of Washington scurried for cover, the soldiers of the Third U.S. Infantry (Old Guard) marched twenty-one steps, turned to face the tomb, pausing twenty-one seconds in respect for soldiers who died for their country "known but to God," and then paced off twenty-one steps in the opposite direction.

Who could not be moved by that tribute?

Christians sometimes resist "soldier language" in the description of their commitment to Jesus Christ. Scripture does not. In fact, terms like *fellow soldier, soldiers of Jesus Christ,* and *armor of God* are embraced, recognizing duty, honor, and sacrifice as some of our most noble human traits.

Our chance to be in fellowship with God was purchased at a terrible cost. The agony of Jesus' prayer in the garden of Gethsemane the night before His death moves us beyond words—or it should. The horrible assault on His physical body by the torturous crucifixion moves us to utterly humbled gratitude—or it should. The unspeakable attack on His divine nature by the heaping of our sins on His sinless self cements our passionate loyalty to whatever duty He calls us to—or it should.

Sixty seconds a minute, sixty minutes an hour, twenty-four hours a day—Christians stand guard over the honor of God, choosing by their actions to glorify Him or to cause Him deep sorrow.

Every breath we take, every job we do, every person we encounter, and every crisis we face brings us a chance to serve God, to honor Him by remembering our duty to Him, to be willing to sacrifice our very existence if His service demands it.

Even in the hurricanes of our lives, when the driving rain of pain and the havoc-wreaking winds of struggle tempt us to seek the shelter of surrender and inaction, a tomb filled and emptied two thousand years ago beckons us to pace our own twenty-one steps, pause to honor Christ, and take the next faithful twenty-one steps of service guarding the glory of the One whose sacrifice gives us eternity.

Grant us strength, O Lord, this very day to persevere, returning honor to Your name in the culture where we serve.

WEEK 9

Keeper of the Lights

Others went out on the sea in ships; they were merchants on the mighty waters. They saw the works of the LORD, his wonderful deeds in the deep. For he spoke and stirred up a tempest that lifted high the waves. They mounted up to the heavens and went down to the depths; in their peril their courage melted away. They reeled and staggered like drunken men; they were at their wits' end. Then they cried out to the LORD in their trouble, and he brought them out of their distress. He stilled the storm to a whisper; the waves of the sea were hushed. They were glad when it grew calm, and he guided them to their desired haven (PSALM 107:23–30 NIV).

THE KEEPER OF THE LIGHT, officially, that cold January night in 1856 was Samuel Burgess. But lighthouse keepers in the early days of the American republic often held two jobs, and Keeper Burgess found it necessary to chase lobsters to feed his family. This meant the keeper of the light, in fact, that cold January night was 17-year-old Abbie Burgess, the keeper's oldest daughter.

Midday, mid-January, midwinter, Keeper Samuel slid his dory in the water and headed off to Rockland, Maine, in search of groceries and much-needed supplies. The lighthouse cutter (ship) that usually delivered supplies to Matinicus Rock in those pre-Civil War days hadn't made it out, and so young Abbie was left to tend two lighthouses on the tiny island twenty-two miles out from the nearest shore. She also watched over her invalid mother and three young sisters.

As if God were writing a Hollywood script, less than four hours after the dory disappeared from sight, the winds shifted, and a nor' easter bore down on the tiny isle.

Lighthouse tending wasn't push buttons and electric generators in those days, especially in the winter, when the oil was likely to grow thick from the cold. Even on good nights Abbie would often have to stay up all night nursing oil into stubborn lamp-wicks. It was the only way ships at sea could be warned of the dangerous ledges waiting to claim lives and cargo.

Day after day, night after night, winds battered the island in one of the worst storms of the nineteenth century. Massive waves crashed against the buildings and towers. The old keeper's dwelling, a wooden structure, yielded first, its splintered bits whipped to sea and scattered miles away along the beaches in Penobscot Bay. Next, the sea crashed into the newer, stronger keeper's home, flooding it and forcing Abbie to move her mother and sisters to the higher of the two towers. Again and again, she sprinted back and forth the sixty yards between the north and south lighthouse towers, each time making the exhausting climb up the flights of stairs to the lamps.

On the seas around her, captains and crews fought their own battles against the sea and the storm, unaware of the drama playing out on Matinicus Rock. All they knew was that two lights shone uninterrupted for four nights, beckoning them to safe harbor even as they warned them what dangers lay between them and their desired haven.

In the logbook Abbie would later write: "Though at times greatly exhausted with my labors, not once did the lights fail. Under God I was able to perform all my accustomed duties as well as my father's."

It was many days before the sea would let Abbie's father return to the island. From a distance, how he must have marveled at the unwavering appearance of those twin beacons so far offshore, knowing in his heart of hearts who was truly tending. How much more must Abbie's heavenly Father have marveled at the majesty, tenacity, and courage of one of His own.

In God's economy, all of us who know His Son as Savior are keepers of the light. While God loves His physical church—those structures and places where we gather to worship and equip ourselves—He does not hide Himself inside those walls. Nor does He want the light we guard to be hidden there either. Like Abbie, we are to be about the Father's business, in brokerages on Wall Street, cubicles in Malaysia, cornfields in Nebraska, or any other job that honors Him.

Like Abbie, that means keeping the light, even when the storms of life threaten to sweep away the things we hold most dear and even when it seems no one else sees or knows what we're doing. Those who live around us are always watching the light we carry. They may poke fun at it in lighter moments, but when the storms of life hit—them or us—their attention turns acutely to the keepers, waiting to see if we're faithful in the storm.

We know intuitively that people pay closer attention to our lives outside the safe harbor of the church. For them, the efficacy of the light of Christ in our lives rests firmly on the stones of competence, integrity, diligence, and compassion. May that light shine through His keepers each workday.

Let the storms of life be our finest hours!

WEEK 10

If Jesus Came Today

For God did not send the Son into the world to judge the world, but that the world might be saved through Him (JOHN 3:17).

IF JESUS CAME TODAY . . .

He would probably visit Gloucester, Massachusetts, to pick up a fisherman or two for His inner circle and then head to China to find an electronics technician to join the group. He'd ask a truck driver in South Australia and a stockbroker in New York before finding two more factory workers in Kenya. None of them would be more deserving of selection than the millions of other workers out there. It's just that Jesus would see something in them nobody else does: an ability to hear and love Him.

In his travels He would likely stop along the way to eat dinner with a modern-day Zaccheus, a CEO or CFO who has bloated the books but hasn't been caught yet. Those of us who have been Christians for years would be disappointed at His choice, and we would be skeptical when the CEO or CFO emerged from his lunch to declare his intent to "put things right."

He would sit for hours with anyone willing to listen but wouldn't stick around long for those seeking to impress Him.

He wouldn't be involved in politics or protests, not because He thought they were wrong or aren't essential but because His brief mission would be narrowly focused on seeing the barrier between people and God; His one goal would be to remove that barrier.

He'd be in church on the Sabbath but in the marketplace on workdays and in homes every evening.

He would tell us that how we do our job is as important as how we worship, that doing more is less important than knowing Him.

He would shame people who tried to shame sinners; then He would turn around and tell the sinners to stop their wrong-doing.

He would give hours and hours to nurse the hurts of relief workers in refugee camps, but He would also spend hours and hours listening to farmers talk about their crops, architects talk about the magic of creating a building in their minds, and anyone else who did their job with joy.

He would mourn the pain of unemployment and be deeply hurt by how little Christians do to help each other.

He would tell workers to stop stealing time from their employers by not giving their best or by loafing when they should be working. He would tell employers to stop stealing time from their workers' families by demanding long hours or telling them to "work 'til the job is finished."

He would stop by our houses to see what we own, then take us to places where people are hurting and ask us what we're doing about it.

He would visit children, and He would have harsh words for those who ignore their physical needs, but He would save His harshest words for those who ignore their spiritual needs.

He wouldn't visit the seats of power, but He'd tell us each to pray for our leaders, even those we don't agree with or don't like.

He would tell us to rest more.

He would celebrate the fifth day of an alcoholic's sobriety and the first day of a sinner's salvation.

He would marvel at the faith of the mother whose child is sick. He would weep at the things sin has caused in creation.

And at the end of it all, having seen our fighting and our sins and our excesses and our obsessions and our self-centeredness and our rebellion, He would step up and do whatever God asked of Him to make it possible for us to know God and to have eternal life—even though that means death and suffering.

. . . Because He loves us that much.

WEEK 11

Workplace Legacies

For to me, to live is Christ and to die is gain (PHILIPPIANS 1:21).

"I REMEMBER!" SHE DECLARED FIRMLY, as she told me a story nearly five decades old. Her eyes lit up and her words rushed out as she talked about a working Christian whose legacy still echoes in her world.

....

Bill Wallace understood in 1935 what some of us still wrestle to grasp: the gifts that make us useful to others also make us useful to God. Wallace was a promising surgeon in Knoxville, Tennessee, when he felt God calling him to take his skills to China. He went, not because it was a romantic gesture and not because he couldn't serve God as a doctor in Knoxville but because it was the place God wanted him.

The concept of sacrifice has slipped away from us. Instead, we seek Scripture passages promising peace; we pray earnestly for security and—all too often—prosperity. We move from place to place in search of the perfect church, the perfect job, the perfect home, the perfect spouse. We wait for God to serve us instead of looking for ways to serve Him, especially in the reality of today's multicultural workplace.

It is difficult in some places to serve God at work. It is tough to reflect His character and His glory when workers around you are swearing and defaming His name or are antagonistic toward or disinterested in Him or your testimony for Him.

Bill Wallace went to China in the 1930s. He braved language barriers, longings for family, and physical danger—all to serve God by serving Chinese citizens in his role as a surgeon. He wasn't great with words; in fact, he had trouble with the language. But his service and his words mixed on the job to win the hearts of a people who had little reason to listen—*until his labors gave them that reason!*

In 1951 the Communists swept up Mainland China, placing Wallace in prison. They trumped up false charges against him but could not find one person to support those charges. Eventually guards in the prison killed him, and the Communist officials quickly buried him without a service or headstone. Braving the wrath of their new rulers, the local Chinese secretly raised funds and erected a monument to him.

Thirty-three years later, Dr. Wallace's remains were returned to his family in Tennessee. Three Chinese doctors secretly asked to see the ashes of their friend before the transfer. One reached out to touch the ashes in a gesture of respect still deeply evident after three decades.

Five nurses from around the globe gathered at the cemetery in Knoxville, Tennessee, one sunny afternoon in 1998. They were there to honor the surgeon they met a half century before when they were young Chinese nursing students. At the cemetery where Wallace rests, they paid to reproduce the monument built in China to remember the man. On both monuments, the words were the same: "For me to live is Christ . . ."

The way we close the deal today, the way we pack those boxes, the way we handle that employee, the way we price our product, the way we tend the patient, the way we teach the child, the way we do whatever we do today leaves a residue of remembrance in the lives of those who meet us.

. . . .

"I remember!" she said, and then she told me a story about a simple doctor whose faithful service changed her eternity long ago. It wasn't his death she discussed, but his life!

What do people remember of us?

WEEK 12

The Reason We Exist

Therefore we do not lose heart, but though our outer man is decaying, yet our inner man is being renewed day by day. For momentary, light affliction is producing for us an eternal weight of glory far beyond all comparison, while we look not at the things which are seen, but at the things which are not seen; for the things which are seen are temporal, but the things which are not seen are eternal (2 CORINTHIANS 4:16–18).

WHAT YOU BELIEVE ABOUT LIFE after death determines how you spend your days.

Well, that's how it works in theory, anyway. In practice, you've probably already discovered that isn't really true. The thrill of the big deal, the press of the big deadline, or the stress of the monthly mortgage often take precedence over thoughts of eternity. In fact, most of us live our lives as if tomorrow won't get here.

That kind of thinking works when things are going well. The fun of the moment, the satisfaction of security, and maybe even the sweet smell of success allure us from thoughts of the Great Beyond.

But when life takes a sharp turn south, short-term perspectives can be quite daunting. Mired in the misery of the moment, we wonder why life isn't fair or worry over when . . . if . . . it's going to change.

That's because for most of us, including most of us who call ourselves Christians, the reason we exist is to serve ourselves. Or to serve our families. Or to serve God. Nothing could be further from the truth. We do not exist to work. We do not exist to evangelize. We do not exist to marry and raise children. We do not exist to make the world a better place.

The reason we exist is to be in fellowship with God.

Until we learn that, until that sticks in our heads and hearts, we are destined to live out this life like yo-yos, delighted when things go well, discouraged when they don't. Until we learn that, most of what we do has little meaning and little lasting effect for the kingdom. Until we learn that, we hurl unintended insult at the work of Jesus Christ, who suffered and died not so we could work, not so we could evangelize, not so we could raise families, not so we could make the world a better place, but so we could once again be in fellowship with God.

Eternity began the moment we were created. Heaven begins the moment we meet Jesus. But contentment and joy will never be ours until we recognize that all of life is about a relationship with God.

When Peter writes that we should be "ready to give an answer for the hope that is in us," he was talking about a hope that comes from knowing and loving God; from trusting Him to balance the scales eventually; a hope that reminds us this isn't all there is to life; that one day all sorrow, all pain, all inequity and misery and trial will no longer be a part of our journey.

But not yet. For now we live in a world messed up by sin and governed by darkness. Or we live in a world made up in our minds, where people are basically good and life is generally comfortable. Measured by any standard but a relationship with God, measured by any standard but the idea that most of our existence will be spent on the other side of death, we are destined to ride a roller-coaster of wows and ows that make little sense but loom large in our vision.

People who don't know Jesus Christ as Savior have no hope, even if they don't understand that yet. But most of us who do know Christ have bought into the idea that life is about doing, about having a mission or a purpose that we can use to measure progress or to feel better.

Jesus sacrificed for one reason: to put us back in touch with God. If the center of our life isn't being in touch with Him, then nothing we do will satisfy the yawning chasm in our soul.

WEEK 13

One Soul at a Time

For this reason also, God highly exalted Him, and bestowed on Him the name which is above every name, so that at the name of Jesus every knee will bow, of those who are in heaven and on earth and under the earth, and that every tongue will confess that Jesus Christ is Lord, to the glory of God the Father (PHILIPPIANS 2:9–11).

WORKING CHRISTIANS OFTEN HEAR A call to "capture the boardrooms for Jesus" or to "transform the marketplace for Christ."

Those missions miss the mark entirely. We should not aspire to be a Christian workplace but rather a workplace filled with Christians. The battle is about character, not culture.

The difference is huge. The distinction is significant. Becoming a Christian workplace focuses our energies on capturing control of an organization or institution, thinking if we control its structure we assure ourselves a God-honoring environment. Unfortunately, experience (and sinful human nature) has taught us the same workplace stresses, struggles, and foibles exist in Christian organizations that are found in corporate workplaces.

We burn off energy targeting influential people because we believe their positions offer us a chance to capture the environments they control. Instead of seeing those influential people as sinners needing Christ (or Christians needing encouragement), we see them as means to an end, tools to be used for objectives we set.

Our goals should always be grassroots in nature, focused on individuals and not institutions. Our objective must always be to introduce others to Christ and to encourage those who already know Christ to grow in their understanding of His call on their lives.

Revival sweeps a culture one person at a time. It starts when an auditor decides she cares so much for the other workers on her team that she swallows her fears and begins to share Christ with them. It grows when a programmer moves alongside another programmer and helps him grow in his budding faith. It is enhanced when Christians in the workplace begin to let their faith influence their individual actions on the job. And revival can really explode when the followers of Christ in a corporation commit themselves to honoring each other rather than fighting the finer points of faith, so others see the bonds that bind and not the dogma that divides.

We do not need a movement that sweeps like a glacier through the culture of our work worlds. We need one person deciding to completely surrender herself to Christ, inspiring one more person to surrender himself completely to Christ, inspiring one more person to surrender . . . and so on.

Then those who don't know Christ will see Christ in us, and some of them will want to know Him, too.

Let our faith today not be governed by a desire to control institutions but by a desire to honor God and a desire to lead coworkers we care about from the terrible fate that awaits them in an eternity separated from Him.

WEEK 14

You Feed Them

When Jesus went ashore, He saw a large crowd, and He felt compassion for them because they were like sheep without a shepherd; and He began to teach them many things. When it was already quite late, His disciples came to Him and said, "This place is desolate and it is already quite late; send them away so that they may go into the surrounding countryside and villages and buy themselves something to eat." But He answered them, "You give them something to eat!" (MARK 6:34–37).

"YOU FEED THEM."

If we're not paying close attention, we miss those words from Jesus. That's because we're so enamored with the five loaves/two fish miracle that we slip right by what Jesus says.

A huge crowd had gathered in a remote area near a lake for one reason only: to see and hear Jesus. As the day wore on, the disciples started getting nervous and began to press Jesus to call the session to a close. "Send them away," the disciples said, "so they can find themselves something to eat."

"*You feed them,*" was Jesus' reply.

The disciples answered Him by explaining the obvious: there wasn't enough food to go around. The rest, as they say, is history. Jesus blessed five loaves of bread and two fish, and then He gave them to the disciples to use to feed the five thousand. It turned out to be more than enough to meet the need. But don't miss this fact: Jesus didn't feed the five thousand; *the disciples did*—just as He had instructed them.

Not too long after that, Jesus did it again in an episode that still confounds savvy marketing and corporate strategists. Sitting by the sea cooking fish in the days after His resurrection, Jesus looked at His tiny band of dispirited disciples and told them He was leaving. They must have dropped their jaws at that news. How could He leave now? Didn't Jesus realize just how hungry people would be to hear the Messiah was alive?

"You feed them," was the answer they would get from Jesus.

He's using those same words today. Whether you're a janitor in Jakarta or a CEO in Cleveland, you have exactly the same assignment in the kingdom of God. Feed His sheep. Literally and figuratively.

Millions of workers without the hope of Christ in their heart. Millions of people without enough food to stay alive. Millions of children without health care. Millions of workers being viewed as interchangeable parts in a mechanized march to prosperity instead of being seen (and treated) as individual bearers of the image of God. Thousands of bosses being badgered and belittled by workers too concerned with themselves to care about a greater good.

In the middle of such great need, we Christians stand and cry out to Jesus to solve these problems, and His answer puzzles and haunts us as it echoes down through time with the consistency of a God who is the same yesterday, today, and forever.

"You feed them," He says, meaning it literally and spiritually.

Our answer surely doesn't surprise Him. "We don't have enough ____ ____." Not enough what? Time, money, compassion, energy?

We're wrong. No worker lacks the resources. No church or ministry lacks the resources, either. When Jesus tells us to feed His children, He already knows what we have at our disposal, and He will bless those five loaves and two fishes until the work He gives us is accomplished.

What we lack is faith and vision, the ability to see that God decided a long time ago to let us do the labor. Beginning this day, even as we pray for those in need around us, listen to what God says in those quiet moments with Him: *"You feed them."*

Then do it.

WEEK 15

Ethan's Story

For what I received I passed on to you as of first importance: that Christ died for our sins according to the Scriptures, that he was buried, that he was raised on the third day according to the Scriptures (1 CORINTHIANS 15:3–4 NIV).

SHORTLY AFTER GIVING BIRTH TO our son, my wife experienced serious complications. As doctors and nurses rushed in, someone handed my son to me and pushed me to a corner. Amidst urgent, sometimes frantic conversations among the members of the medical team, I heard Cheryl saying quietly, "I'm going . . ."

There wasn't a thing I could do to help her.

Minutes later, one of the nurses noticed my son was turning blue in my arms. Another team of doctors and another team of nurses took Ethan to yet another room.

There wasn't a thing I could do to help him.

Hours later, Cheryl watched as a neonatal intensive care team took her baby to yet another hospital. For all she knew, this was goodbye.

There wasn't a thing she could do to help him.

When I arrived with Ethan at the other hospital, a doctor pulled me aside to tell me it wasn't likely Ethan would survive the next few hours. Hour after hour I sat with my arm reaching into the Isolette unit, rubbing his back and singing to him, not wanting him to be alone if indeed these were his only moments with us. I sang and prayed, praying too for Cheryl, who had the harder night, fighting a lonely battle not only to recover but also unable to be with her little boy.

Hour after hour, Ethan held on.

I remember vividly the moment when a doctor pulled me out of the nursery to tell me he was now sure Ethan would survive. It was Ethan's third day on earth. Even the nurses were crying.

Resurrection is a real event in our household, painted forever in our hearts by a Son who died so a dad could rejoice at the life of a son who did not.

May Passion week, the most important week in the history of humanity, bring us face to face with the One whose suffering we caused, and may that face-to-face encounter bring us closer to understanding the full measure of His love and mercy.

He is risen indeed!

WEEK 16

Legacies

....

Therefore, since we have so great a cloud of witnesses surrounding us, let us also lay aside every encumbrance and the sin which so easily entangles us, and let us run with endurance the race that is set before us, fixing our eyes on Jesus, the author and perfecter of faith (HEBREWS 12:1–2A).

WE WERE ROLLING THROUGH THE hills where Jesse James once roamed, six of us crammed in a car meant for five. Ahead of us, a hearse carried my pastor.

Riding in the car to the cemetery, I resented the normal chatter among the others. It felt disrespectful. I wanted them to be sullen, withdrawn, contemplative. I wanted them to feel sad the same way I felt sad, to mourn the way I mourned. Ahead of us lay the body of a man whose whole life had been devoted to Christ, whose every waking hour seemed to be spent serving the neighbors Christ commands us to serve. At nineteen, I wasn't wise enough yet to understand that people manage mourning in different ways. All I knew was my pastor was gone, and the world didn't seem to notice.

I was only seven when I met Francis. He was the quintessential rural Baptist preacher, spewing fire and brimstone from the pulpit in a voice that surely shook the gates of hell itself. It was scary, to be sure. But oh, when he stepped down from that pulpit! Never a human exhibited more the gentleness of Christ than burly old Francis. Every fiber of my faith traces its roots to the hours he spent teaching me truth.

For years he walked beside me, teaching me Christianity belonged in the workplace as much as the pulpit, that how I lived said more than how I talked. Every time he sensed me wavering, he nudged me back to Scripture, calling me back to the one place where truth may be reliably re-learned. Far too often, though, the memory of our chats has been drowned out by the seductive call to do something big, be somebody big, producing a desire to be served instead of serving.

What I didn't realize all those years is that Francis wasn't planting *his* wisdom in my head. The words he spoke, the wisdom he offered—all came from his own relationship with Christ. He modeled intimacy with God by mentoring me. He hid Scripture in the corners of my life, knowing what I didn't know then: that once planted in our heads, God's truth never really leaves us, even when we try to push it out of the way.

We were not just meant to be mentored. Younger faces look to us to model something as their mentors, to pass on what we've learned from our journey. What wisdom are they hearing from our words? What truth do they see reflected in the paths we choose? What echoes are we planting in the recesses of their hearts? Are we hiding *our* thoughts in their heads, or are we passing on to them the wisdom of God?

Riding down a bumpy country road that day so long ago, I noticed a pickup pulling over as our line of cars approached. A farmer stepped out of his truck, pulled off his hat, and stood silently as we passed. The chatter in the car stopped short at this unexpected moment of tribute, and the snapshot of that farmer with his hat in his hand etched itself forever in my head.

May the memory of those who brought us to Christ renew our commitment to live as they would want us to live—for Him. May we find, in our own circle, coworkers and family members whose lives wait for words God gives us to share, and may we make the time to not only share them but live them.

WEEK 17

It's That Moment

He who dwells in the shelter of the Most High will abide in the shadow of the Almighty. I will say to the LORD, "My refuge and my fortress, my God, in whom I trust!" (PSALM 91:1–2).

IT'S THAT MOMENT WHEN YOU realize your aging parent no longer knows who you are . . . when your company tells you you're no longer needed . . . when someone you love is gravely ill . . .

It's the moment when depression makes one more hour seem unbearable to contemplate . . . when your loved one passes . . . when your own physical pain incapacitates you . . .

It's the moment when you wake up and realize none of what you've done in life has glorified God . . . when failure confronts you . . . when you can't pay your bills . . .

It's that moment when your children cry out and you can't help them . . . when your children rebel . . . when your children leave this earth before you . . .

It's the moment when the soul of the one you care for passes into eternity, and you have no assurance he or she ever met Christ.

It's the moment when the pain of the struggles of life seems more than you can bear.

It is in that moment you most need to hear God has not forgotten you. It is in that moment that you most need to hear the echo of His voice as it whispers, "It will not always be this way."

We cannot adequately explain the hardest moments of our lives. We cannot soothe all the sorrows that regularly beset us or the sorrows of those whom God has placed around us. We cannot wave a magic wand and fix the distresses we see besieging those we love, those we work with, those we know.

In our hardest moments, our best efforts are feeble . . . our best words are hollow.

In those moments, it is left for us but to pray, to move alongside each other, and to remind each other in the middle of the storms of life that it will not always be like this.

We who know Christ have a hope beyond the present struggle. Though that knowledge of an eternity may seem distant in this moment, its reality echoes in the back of our minds even as we reel at the crisis before us. Never think that Jesus doesn't see you, isn't listening, isn't longing for that moment when it no longer is this way for any of His children.

When we see you in these moments, we will pray for you, plead for calm in the middle of the trial, and seek God's wisdom in ways to help. We will ask for immediate comfort, ever mindful of the hard realities of a fallen world that means some comforts wait for heaven.

But know this for certain: It will not always be like this . . .

WEEK 18

Still Standing

And when Jesus entered Capernaum, a centurion came to Him, imploring Him, and saying, "Lord, my servant is lying paralyzed at home, fearfully tormented." Jesus said to him, "I will come and heal him." But the centurion said, "Lord, I am not worthy for You to come under my roof, but just say the word, and my servant will be healed (MATTHEW 8:5–9).

EARTHQUAKES RARELY HAPPEN ON SUNDAYS.

You know it's true. The big events that shake our lives don't happen on the days when we're in God's house, where the skilled counselors are standing in our midst waiting with their wise words. Even the little events that shake our lives tend to happen to us when we're away from our symbols of strength and our sources of wisdom.

When the earthquakes are big enough, as in the head-spinning disappearance of jobs and livelihoods, everyone is flattened. When the earthquakes are even bigger, as in the loss of loved ones, we're not only flattened but find it difficult to get back up. Those events stop us in our tracks, and we're more aware of each other, of our common frailties.

Every day, people we work with are flattened by private earthquakes. Health. Finances. Troubled marriages. Loss of loved ones. Fears of job loss. Tyrannical bosses. Sabotage-minded subordinates. Relentless demands. The battles of Joe from the next cubicle or Martha from the next office mix with our own battles, and we feel weak or inadequate in the face of them. We wish we could find a pastor or a "stronger" Christian to tell us what to say or how to act.

Our pastors and our church staff are often excellent sources of strength, but they aren't in our workplaces where the "triage" is taking place. Every day you and I are the representatives God selects to send to the jobsite to point to Him. When the battles start and people are looking around to see who's still standing, it's supposed to be us. We take our faith to the job not just so it can help us cope with what comes our way. We take it with us so it reflects His character, a lighthouse standing against the waves of personal struggle, a beacon to people being swept away by the relentless pace and unending emptiness of a world away from Him.

The centurion in our Scripture passage was a Roman officer, a figure of authority in a conquering army. In this passage from Matthew, this "leader of many" cared enough about the one working for him to go to Jesus. The characteristics that made him go to Christ must be present in us: compassion, humility, and faith. We must cultivate these daily, nourish them in our Sundays, and reflect them in our Tuesdays.

When the witnesses are watching to see who's still standing, make it be you... make it be me.

WEEK 19

Courage, Character, and Civility

If I speak in the tongues of men and of angels, but have not love, I am only a resounding gong or a clanging cymbal. If I have the gift of prophecy and can fathom all mysteries and all knowledge, and if I have a faith that can move mountains, but have not love, I am nothing. If I give all I possess to the poor and surrender my body to the flames, but have not love, I gain nothing (1 CORINTHIANS 13:1–3 NIV).

IT WAS A MOMENT THAT took nearly twenty years of unbelievable sacrifice to manufacture, and even then it would be another twenty-six years before the real celebration could begin.

Still, it was a moment for the ages.

In 1807, Britain's Solicitor-General Samuel Romilly stood to deliver a speech before the House of Commons on the matter of ending the practice of slave trading in the British Empire. In his usual place that evening, William Wilberforce watched the proceedings unfold with a lifetime of emotion sweeping through him. Here, in this very same hall in 1789, Wilberforce had first proposed the unthinkable: that the British Empire should not engage in, nor allow, the practice of slavery.

From the moment he first spoke up, Wilberforce became one of the most hated men in the history of the British Empire. No thinking man, common wisdom declared, could believe an empire can be maintained without slavery. His foes would be found in the royal family, among his fellow parliamentarians, and among the elite of British history. Even Admiral Lord Nelson, he of British Royal Navy heroics, publicly yearned for the chance to do battle against Wilberforce on the matter of slavery.

Wilberforce wasn't attacked just verbally, either, but physically as well. In the face of such formidable opposition, Wilberforce wrote in his diary,

"God Almighty has set before me two great objects, the suppression of the Slave Trade and the reformation of manners."

In other words, not only was Wilberforce intent on destroying one of history's greatest evils, but he intended to do so in a way that rejected returning hate for hate, vitriolic volley for vitriolic volley. He further argued that social reform not based on faith carried the flaws of humanity into those reforms, ultimately hurting the very people needing help. So he set about to make it fashionable to believe in Jesus Christ again, a first step, he argued, in any society wanting to help the weak and oppressed.

So on that vaunted night in 1807, two miracles occurred. First, even before Solicitor General Romilly finished his speech, Wilberforce's peers were on their feet pointing to him and cheering in the boisterous fashion known only to British politicians. One of his peers took it up a notch, and the dignity of the British Empire dissolved into an emotional chorus of hurrahs surely heard in the most distant corners of heaven.

William Wilberforce, once Britain's most hated man, sat quietly in his seat, tears streaming down his cheeks as one after another after another parliamentarian cast a yes vote, ending slave trading 283–16.

Still, much work remained. While slave trading was now illegal, slavery and slave ownership were not. Back to work the *evangelical* Wilberforce went, a man led to Christ (in God's ironic majesty) by former slave trader John Newton, the author of the haunting hymn "Amazing Grace." Wilberforce himself would often declare that before meeting Christ, he lived and served only himself, and after meeting Christ, he lived and served the oppressed.

Again, Wilberforce and his allies refused the easy path of partisan rancor and incivility in public debate. While Americans took up arms to settle the matter in the disastrous and tragic American Civil War, England finished the job on the selfsame floor of the House of Commons. Believing that how he changed culture was as important as the changes themselves, Wilberforce set a course any leader in any culture could follow—if only he or she had the courage and patience to do so.

At long last, on July 26, 1833, colleagues raced to approve the Act of Emancipation, forever abolishing slavery and slave ownership from the

British Empire. Across town, too ill to be present for this final victory in the most important work of his life, the joyous news was delivered to England's best-loved citizen. His earthly work finished, William Wilberforce went to meet the Savior face to face.

In an age ravaged by sinful actions stamped with the human signature of legality, it is not enough for Christians to stand against the stream of culture. In standing, we must also bring honor to the One whose name we carry, finding ways to change hearts and minds instead of looking for new enemies on the horizon.

Courage, character, and civility matter. In the lives of those who seek to represent Jesus Christ, that trio of traits must surely be viewed as inseparable.

WEEK 20

Talking about God at Work

[Jesus said,] "Therefore everyone who confesses Me before men, I will also confess him before My Father who is in heaven. But whoever denies Me before men, I will also deny him before My Father who is in heaven" (MATTHEW 10:32–33).

HERE ARE TEN THINGS ALL Christians should consider as they sort out how to talk about God at work.

1. People only want what looks better to them than what they already have—meaning Christians need to reflect characteristics that demonstrate the joy, peace, and practicality of their faith.
2. Listening is a better testimony than action. When people talk about their trials, stop offering immediate solutions and don't suggest that believing in Jesus will solve all their struggles. Offering immediate solutions only makes people feel stupid or makes them feel like you've reduced their complex issue to a simplistic one. It's insensitive and impractical in most instances to offer easy fixes to people's problems. And while Jesus is the ultimate answer to all of our trials, accepting Him as Savior should never be used as an easy fix to life's pressures.
3. Don't make the Christian faith about doing the right thing; make it about Jesus Christ. There are a lot of people from other faiths (and even no faith) who live ethical lives. We Christians don't have a corner on ethics; we have an answer to eternity: grace.
4. The newer you are in a job, the less you should exercise your right to talk about God.

5. The longer you're in a job, the greater the responsibility you have to share Jesus Christ with your coworkers.
6. You need to know the "second ten words." Most of us know the sound-bite version of our faith, but when people ask us questions, they discover we don't know why we believe what we believe. In other words, there's little depth to our faith, and it shows. There's a reason the Bible says "Study to show thyself approved unto God, a workman who needeth not to be ashamed" (2 Timothy 2:15 KJ21).
7. Don't make sharing your faith about living a good life in front of others; make it about caring enough about others to take risks to change their eternity.
8. Think about the eternal destiny of the difficult people in your workplace. It's often the only way to get past the annoying things they do.
9. Never share your faith when doing so disrupts the workflow.
10. Stop witnessing to people who ask you to stop.

WEEK 21

Sometimes, Rest

Come to Me, all who are weary and heavy-laden, and I will give you rest. Take My yoke upon you and learn from Me, for I am gentle and humble in heart, and you will find rest for your souls. For My yoke is easy and My burden is light (MATTHEW 11:28–30).

WE SERVE A GOD WHO loves us more than our labors.

Certainly God never delights in laziness. He demands we work to feed our families. He expects us to be responsible stewards of the world He created. He expects us to remember that what He gives us as resources are tools to be used in serving Him and not rewards to be hoarded for our own satisfaction.

Certainly He expects us not to be satisfied as long as there are weak, hungry, naked, thirsty, and broken people around us. He expects us never to be satisfied when there are people around us who have not yet responded to the Spirit's tug on their lives.

"From everyone who has been given much," His Word tells us, "much will be required" (Luke 12:28).

And yet we serve a God who loves us more than our labors.

The reason we exist is to be in fellowship with God. We must never forget this because there will be times in our lives when everything else is taken away from us, when the things we love most disappear or we aren't able to serve Him in the ways we always have right now. It is in those hours that He wants us to remember that He loves us not for what we do for Him but because we are His children. We are never strong enough or good enough to earn His salvation, and we are never strong enough or good enough to merit keeping it on our own. It is given to us by receiving the free gift of grace made possible by the work of Jesus Christ.

For those of us who call on the name of Christ for salvation, nothing will ever again separate us from the love of Christ and the fellowship of God.

So even though He wants us to work and even though He desires excellence and rewards perseverance and diligence, what He values most is us.

When all we can do or all we have is taken from us, then all He wants us to do is rest in Him. If this is your condition today, then know this: God is honored by your willingness to rest in Him.

Even warriors get tired.

WEEK 22

Making a Difference at Work

Bear one another's burdens, and thereby fulfill the law of Christ
(GALATIANS 6:2).

BARCELONA OLYMPICS, 1992. FOUR-HUNDRED METER semifinals. British racer Derek Redmond is lying on the ground, having collapsed when his hamstring snapped nearly halfway through the race. Thousands and thousands of people in the stands gasp as he refuses the stretcher-bearers and tries to stand. Millions of television viewers stop in their tracks as they realize he is going to try to finish the race by hobbling on one good leg the last 250 meters.

What happened next remains one of the most memorable scenes in sports history. One spectator couldn't just sit. Racing out of the stands, dodging officials and medics and security guards, Derek's father makes an improbable trek from his seat to his son's side on the track. Together, the two stay in the lane, stay on the track, and finish the race. The stunned crowd, weepy with the emotion of this most human of moments, roars its thunderous approval as Redmond crosses the finish line.

Few people, I suspect, remember the names of the seven other runners in that race. What we remember is the disappointment of a race cut short, the determination of a racer to finish what he started, and the overpowering love of a father.

Every single day in this ministry, we are confronted with men and women whose races are cut short by the trials of life. Facing daunting circumstances, they stagger back to their feet in often lonely vigils, determined not to be sidelined by the crises they face. It would be easier, I think, if their drama were played out before cheering throngs of caring Christians, eager to encourage them in their journey. It would be easier, too, if the arms of the Father could be felt tangibly wrapping around them as they continued their trek.

But sometimes God's presence can't be felt so tangibly; sometimes His voice can't be heard so audibly. Sometimes the cheering crowds are so focused on the winners in the race that the struggling runners go unnoticed.

Readers often ask for suggestions on how to shape their workplace for Christ. Here, then, are some concrete places to look. Who among you is struggling? Is there a single parent barely managing to keep pace with life? Are there people in your department having trouble understanding their jobs? Are there people in your circle without jobs, in need of referrals, networking, and even coaching? Has someone failed miserably, and even now others are piling on them like the Pharisees, ready to stone the woman caught in adultery? Has technology made an older worker obsolete? Has alcohol, drugs, or overwork laid claim to a coworker? Is there illness, injury, or loss raging through the life of the worker in cubicle number 7? God is indeed honored by our competence, integrity, and achievement when these things are offered as sacrifices to Him, as testimonies to His glory. Working well, laboring diligently, and stretching ourselves to tend His creation demonstrate to those around us the source of our strength and remind a fallen world that God is triumphant.

But more often than not, it is in those quieter moments, when we stop to wrap ourselves around a coworker, that the silent witnesses to the effects of our faith are best able to see God. Never be more concerned with the product than the people. Never forget that in the race for eternity, every one of us has fallen and cannot get up. When we remember the arms of grace enveloping us as we fight the good fight, as we struggle to finish the race, let us demonstrate that grace to others in equally tangible ways.

Then perhaps the changes we wish for in the places where we work may in fact slip silently into place.

WEEK 23

A Leader Like That

Then [Jesus] said to them, "My soul is deeply grieved, to the point of death; remain here and keep watch with Me." And He went a little beyond them, and fell on His face and prayed, saying, "My Father, if it is possible, let this cup pass from Me; yet not as I will, but as You will." And He came to the disciples and found them sleeping (MATTHEW 26:38-40A).

HE PICKED HIS OWN TEAM, and still every one of them failed Him.

They jockeyed for position, questioned His objective, misunderstood His priorities, and failed to comprehend the central purpose of His work. In the end, one of them sold Him out for reasons we still don't fully comprehend, and every one of the others deserted Him when given the chance to be faithful.

Still, remember, He picked them.

So He waded patiently through their questions, even when those questions showed how little they knew of the labor they shared with Him. He protected them from the storms that beset them. He trained them carefully, always focused not on the failures of the moment but rather on that moment in the future when the mission finally made its way from His lips to their heads and hearts. He watched them fail on training runs and patiently trained them some more.

Maybe He should have picked better people. Or maybe He should have replaced them when it was clear they failed to grasp the mission of the work.

It would seem especially true, given their inability to pick up signs of the crisis building at Jerusalem. Tired from the work and the emotions constantly swirling around from being alongside Him, they even failed to keep Him company in His darkest hours.

And, when He most needed their support, they were gone. Like mist at midday, they disappeared when He was threatened and watched from a distance while He carried on without them.

Dejected, disconsolate, and reeling, they gathered after His death without any idea of what to do next.

And then He did something most remarkable. He picked them again!

Jesus could have returned triumphant before Caesar; could have taunted the Roman soldiers who crucified Him and the high priests who belittled Him. Instead, He went back to the people who failed and picked them again.

This time they understood. Armed not only with the information He gave them before His triumph but now with the wisdom to put it in perspective, they did what they could not have done before: They built His church. We who know Him today stand as fruit of their labors, heirs to their strength.

Now, in the places where we work, a new generation of laborers has been called. For reasons we can't quite comprehend, He has plucked us out of the morass of sinful selfishness and chosen us to join His labors.

With the same quiet patience He exhibited toward His first twelve, He trains us for the effort. And when we falter, when we let the irritations of life or the crises before us distract us from the tasks He assigns us, He does something few managers are likely to do: He picks us again!

How can we not serve a leader like that?

WEEK 24

Hard to Lead from the Rear

Then Mordecai told them to reply to Esther, "Do not imagine that you in the king's palace can escape any more than all the Jews. For if you remain silent at this time, relief and deliverance will arise for the Jews from another place and you and your father's house will perish. And who knows whether you have not attained royalty for such a time as this?" (ESTHER 4:13–14).

A TROUBLING TRUTH HAUNTS THE world of marketplace ministry. While much of its resources are aimed at leaders—the so-called movers and shakers of culture—this target audience is usually AWOL when it comes to the hard work of bringing God to the job.

While large groups of men and women gather to eagerly discover how best to use their careers and their workplaces to honor Him, one segment of the population is notable by its absence. When small groups of men and women gather to study what Scripture has to say about faith and work, that same segment of the workplace population is often absent again.

It's hard to lead from the rear.

To be certain, workplace surveys teach us that the more educated, the more successful people are, the less likely they are to embrace the Christian faith. Jesus even indicates this in His famous "camel through the eye of a needle" passage, where He acknowledges that the more we have, the more it can distract from the eternal, the truly important. Still, in the corridors of power, the corner offices, and the boardrooms, there are mighty men and women of God who know and love Christ but choose to be silent about Him in the very place where He has sent them to serve. They forget that God placed them in positions of influence for a reason.

Just as demoralizing, though, is the realization that often when these leaders of our culture decide they will participate in activities that exercise their faith, they choose to do so only among their peers in Bible studies, audiences, and congregations where others on their own professional level are present. Affinity is attractive, but its seductive comfort places leaders with other leaders instead of among the people God wants them to encourage and inspire. Rather than taking up the lead as shepherds, these captains of industry reduce themselves to being merely another sheep, albeit in a more comfortable setting.

It's hard to lead from the rear.

Working Christians honor God best by making their whole lives His possession. The single mother working two jobs still finds time to sit in Bible studies in the office because she hopes the places that take her away from her children are valuable in God's eyes, but she's not sure. Busyness does not keep her from taking time out for Bible study and shouldn't be used as an excuse for those who are called to lead her, either. She should look to her left or her right and see not just her peers but her captains of industry and be encouraged by their humility, their vulnerability, and their presence.

Pastors and churches are called to equip us to live our lives for God in the workplace and the home and the culture. They are the only leaders who are assigned to the rear. The rest of us are sent to the front lines of creation to do the daily work that makes up the world that God still rules. And when God calls you to leadership roles in those front lines, then He calls you not to silence, not to absence, but to be out in front in faith as well.

It's time to come out of the palace. Like Mordecai reminded Esther, "Who knows whether you have not attained royalty for such a time as this?"

WEEK 25

It Ought to Be Easier

Therefore, since we are surrounded by such a great cloud of witnesses, let us throw off everything that hinders and the sin that so easily entangles, and let us run with perseverance the race marked out for us. Let us fix our eyes on Jesus, the author and perfecter of our faith, who for the joy set before him endured the cross, scorning its shame, and sat down at the right hand of the throne of God. Consider him who endured such opposition from sinful men, so that you will not grow weary and lose heart (HEBREWS 12:1–3 NIV).

"IT OUGHT TO BE EASIER than it is . . . "

I heard that from Brian on the construction site after he spent ten hours laying rebar for a supervisor who thought screaming was a motivational tool. I heard it, too, from Marian, who was about to announce the closing of the plant that had been the working home of many, some for as long as thirty-seven years. I heard those same words from claims adjuster Joseph, who was there to tell me my worker's daughter's illness wasn't covered; from Lillian, whose four children under thirteen fended for themselves while she worked two jobs to feed, house, and clothe them. I hear it regularly from Christians blindsided by stressful jobs, even though they're living faithful lives.

"It ought to be easier than it is..."

How many times have Christians collapsed under the weight of reality when they finally discover that "the rain falls on the just and the unjust?" Shouldn't there be some tangible, get-ahead-in-life benefit to being a follower of Jesus Christ? Even among serious working Christians, there is often a Don Quixote search going on for a world-and-life view that makes us completely at rest in the work of our hands.

It really *ought to be* easier than it is. But for most of us, though, that's never going to happen. We need to get our arms around it.

Once sin messed up human beings, it messed up the rest of creation also. Suddenly, tornados and hurricanes and earthquakes and floods ravaged a garden intended to be free of those things. Suddenly, relationships that were meant to be unbroken and continuous weren't unbroken, weren't continuous. Suddenly, where death wasn't planned, death became real. Cancer, influenza, AIDS, car wrecks, terrorist attacks, war, and all the other forms of death that visit humans weren't originally part of creation. They were added when sin was added. Work, too, was burdened with the weight and impact of sin.

When we humans let sin into God's kingdom, here's how He altered work: *"Cursed is the ground because of you; through painful toil you will eat of it all the days of your life. It will produce thorns and thistles for you, and you will eat the plants of the field. By the sweat of your brow you will eat your food until you return to the ground, since from it you were taken; for dust you are and to dust you will return"* (Genesis 3:17–19 NIV).

Still, most of us live hoping we can be exceptions to this story. Indeed, all of us think we can point to people whose lives and work made them pre-fall workers instead of post-fall workers. When our real lives fall short of our dreams or fall short of what we think others have, we grow discouraged and disenchanted. We think we're doing something wrong or that God is not holding up His end of the bargain.

After all, we think, *God owes us…*

And *that's* when we get into trouble. Until we understand *we* owe *God*, then all we do will seem like rolling massive stones up steep hills with no help. Every trial, every heartbreak, every setback, every stressful moment will challenge our faith. God Himself is saying to us that it "ought to be easier than this," and so He offers assurances in Revelation that one day it will be; work will indeed be restored to its pre-fall joyous state. But He does us one better than that: Rather than leaving us alone in the muck we've created, He promises His presence to help us persevere, indeed to help us move toward a pre-fall work experience, even though it can never fully be reached, just as He helps us move toward a pre-fall sanctification that will never be fully achieved this side of eternity. We hear it in the words of David in the Twenty-third Psalm or in the majestic lilt of Psalm 8, but we hear it most vividly in the words of Jesus when He says, *"Come to Me, all you who labor and are heavy laden, and I will give you rest"* (Matthew 11:28 NKJV).

We must stop hunting for stress-free journeys and look instead to how our time here can be an expression of gratitude for the restoration Christ promises to those who call upon His name. Then, in whatever circumstance we find ourselves, every act can be redemptive, every job can be an expression that adds value to His creation because our eyes are on Him and not on ourselves.

Then we can echo Paul when he writes in Philippians 1:21: *"For to me, to live is Christ and to die is gain."*

WEEK 26

Compensation

They came to Capernaum; and when [Jesus] was in the house, He began to question [his disciples], "What were you discussing on the way?" But they kept silent, for on the way they had discussed with one another which of them was the greatest. Sitting down, He called the twelve and said to them, "If anyone wants to be first, he shall be last of all and servant of all" (MARK 9:33–35).

HOW MUCH IS ENOUGH FOR our needs? When does what we accept in our compensation package define our compassion for our workers?

At mealtime in the Yup'ik Eskimo culture, fathers eat first, then elders, and women and children eat last. The same is true of cultures as far-flung as India, Zambia, and Samoa.

Imagine being a father in such a culture, especially a culture where food is scarce. Each meal is an opportunity for you to teach your children. Would you teach them sacrifice and the depths of your love by taking only what you need to keep your strength? Or would you teach them less savory truths about humanity? To be sure, as these cultures established their customs, it was necessary for the father to eat first to sustain his strength to bring in tomorrow's meal. But aid workers now tell us gluttony sets in, and the practice often leaves little food for women and children in poor areas of the world.

The love of a father for his wife and children is defined each meal by the amount of food taken from the family table.

Westerners will likely be uncomfortable using this concept as a strategy for setting compensation, and maybe rightfully so. After all, it is abundantly clear the "carrot" at the end of the "stick" prompts incredible progress in our economic systems.

Still, there is a kernel of usefulness to the concept, especially for Christian men and women who want to lead like Jesus. Are there opportunities for us to take only what we need in order to assure that the newest worker in the firm has a living wage?

For men and women who follow Christ, every area of their lives is an opportunity to teach others about Him. Leaders and managers who indulge themselves *at the expense of their companies or their employees* demonstrate a life of service to self over others, ignoring the sacrificial example Christ set during His time on earth.

To be certain, leadership is lonely and can often be taxing. And the complex responsibilities of leadership *do* merit special consideration when it comes to sorting out compensation issues. Still, Christian managers/owners must carefully consider the employees God gives them to shepherd before they decide *how much is enough for their own compensation.*

Resisting the serve-me-first principle isn't just useful in compensation areas either. Parents with chaotically busy schedules face similar serve-me-first dilemmas when sorting out priorities and the demands of careers versus the needs of their families.

Truth is, each of us faces the kinds of choices fathers in these men-eat-first cultures face. How we behave in those moments defines our compassion and our understanding of the servant leadership to which Jesus calls us all.

WEEK 27

A Work/Faith Journey, Part 1

Therefore I urge you, brethren, by the mercies of God, to present your bodies a living and holy sacrifice, acceptable to God, which is your spiritual service of worship. And do not be conformed to this world, but be transformed by the renewing of your mind, so that you may prove what the will of God is, that which is good and acceptable and perfect (Romans 12:1–2).

Divide and conquer.

That strategy works in nearly every area of life. Warriors use it to overcome a larger enemy force. Parents use it to help children swamped with homework. Workers use it to make mammoth assignments more manageable.

Our work/faith journey is no different. Sitting in a pew on Sunday morning, you may hear the pastor challenging you to "surrender completely to God." Or you may have heard us in this weekly writing call ourselves and others to surrender to Jesus Christ as Lord of the workplace.

But how? Where do we start? Some would argue that we simply need to "let go and let God" have His way with us. That seems simple enough, except it doesn't work that way for most people. Those to whom God gives the gift of faith can indeed simply yield and find the Holy Spirit takes command. If you're one of those granted this gift, you are surely blessed. Be warned, though, that each gift also carries with it responsibility. If you're granted the gift of faith, God expects you to hit the ground with your feet already moving.

For the rest of us, faith is a constant struggle, a radio wave that comes in and out based on the stuff life tosses into the mix. Some days we feel good about our relationship with God, others not so good. We need spiritual mile markers we can point to in our journey that remind us of our progress. Consider these mile markers in the work/faith journey:

1. Clearing the decks: Overcoming the clutter in our life that prevents us from hearing God. This stage requires that we shift our lives from being driven by ambition and achieve a healthy work ethic. Incumbent on reaching this first mile marker is our ability to define success God's way, discover balance, understand how much money and authority is enough, and when and how to rest. It is remembering that we were created to be in relationship with God and that work is merely one facet of that relationship. Our identity is in Christ, not what we do.

2. Changing our moral compass: The next stage in the spiritual journey is discovering that right and wrong are not subject to circumstance or culture but are established by God. Doing what is right in our own eyes is not sufficient; we must understand what God defines as holy and correct and must work to line our lives up with His standards (not line others up—line ourselves up!). Too many of us work on the speck in our neighbors' eyes while ignoring the log in our own. In this stage, we must learn to deal with difficult people, resolve conflict, develop our commitment to honesty and character, and develop our compassionate codes of conduct, all in ways that are gracious and consistent with His commands.

3. Talking about God at work: This is often the most difficult stage in the journey because it involves risk. Up to this point, we've been focused on changing us; now God calls us to care about those who don't yet know Him. In this stage, we must discover ways to talk about Him to people who are preoccupied with success (or survival). We must find ways to describe our relationship with Christ that use language our coworkers understand, and we must do so without disrupting the flow of work, ours or anyone else's. This requires intentional action on our part; it does not always come by inspiration or divine appointment.

Our work need not be a series of disconnected trips to nowhere, doing little more than serving our physical needs and our competitive juices. While God asks for only a portion of our material blessings (tithes and offerings), He wants all of us, all of our time and attention. Turning our working selves into co-laborers with Christ requires that we mark out our paths. In the days when our faith is challenged, we may look upon the markers for encouraging signs that the journey is not for naught.

Next week we'll explore three more mile markers in the path from self-absorbed, naïve believers to mature followers surrendered to God's economy.

WEEK 28

A Work/Faith Journey, Part 2

If it is disagreeable in your sight to serve the LORD, choose for yourselves today whom you will serve: whether the gods which your fathers served which were beyond the River, or the gods of the Amorites in whose land you are living; but as for me and my house, we will serve the LORD (JOSHUA 24:15).

No servant can serve two masters; for either he will hate the one and love the other, or else he will be devoted to one and despise the other. You cannot serve God and wealth (LUKE 16:13).

LAST WEEK WE DEFINED THREE spiritual mile markers in a journey from being self-absorbed workers to laborers whose working lives are surrendered completely to the will of God in their jobs. These first three signposts of growth included: (1) a shift from being driven by ambition to achieving a healthy work ethic; (2) a shift from moral relativity to steadfast character; and (3) a shift from spiritual silence to understanding our duty to share our faith in every area of our lives. This week we move through the final three markers.

1. Understanding that the One we live for determines our focus: Especially in Western cultures, the glory of the individual is hyped, creating a "grab-all-you-can-get" mentality in some or a "get-mine-first" in others. The sacrifice of Christ purchased our souls and, therefore, our service. This means that a significant mile marker in our journey of faith must be a shift from self-indulgent lifestyles to lives lived with a purpose. In other words, we must choose where we work by how it fits into God's redemptive plan and not by our own goals and objectives. Doing so requires

understanding how we hear God, how we manage the resources He gives us, and changing how we make decisions and how we discipline ourselves both physically and spiritually.

2. The fifth marker in the journey is a shift from striving to advance ourselves or our culture to affecting that culture Christianly by applying in practical ways the principles of Scripture. Here we begin to challenge the worldviews of those who argue there is no place for God at the office or on the job. We begin to study Scripture with the realization that the One who *created* work also offers wisdom in *doing* work.

3. The final stage in the journey of faith is characterized by having a Christ-centered calling—in other words, measuring our daily labor by how it advances the gates of the kingdom of God in a culture resistant to its influence. In this stage, we learn how to alter course in the changing seasons of our lives, when to serve sacrificially, and when to charge forward boldly. This is the place where we spend ourselves and our resources guided by an intimate relationship with God, not yielding to the seductive lure of cultural reward or the confusing noise of self-absorption. This is where we remind ourselves that the reason we exist is to be in relationship with God, and whether we're sixteen or sixty, eternity is merely beginning. This is the place where we truly surrender to the lordship of Christ.

We must not grow impatient with ourselves in this journey. The enemies of faith and the enemy of God seek to confuse and discourage working Christians. They claim faith is a private matter with no place in culture or work. God declares "I will be exalted (Psalm 46:10)," and He expects us to be the ambassadors of His kingdom in every corner of creation, be it cubicles or corner offices, farm fields, truck cabs, classrooms, or laboratories.

A walk with God is never a ride; it is always an intentional event measured step by step. When we stumble, He lifts us back up and expects us to start forward again. ("For a righteous man falls seven times, and rises again" [Proverbs 24:16].) The joy of the journey is never in outcomes; it's always in the journey itself. It's why Jesus' words to the disciples long ago ring so poignantly in our ears today: "And lo, I am with you always, even to the end of the age" (Matthew 28:20).

WEEK 29

More Than We Can Bear

Who will separate us from the love of Christ? Will tribulation, or distress, or persecution, or famine, or nakedness, or peril, or sword? . . . But in all these things we overwhelmingly conquer through Him who loved us. For I am convinced that neither death, nor life, nor angels, nor principalities, nor things present, nor things to come, now powers, nor height, nor depth, nor any other created thing, will be able to separate us from the love of God, which is in Christ Jesus our Lord (ROMANS 8:35, 37–39).

SOMETIMES, LIFE IS NOT ABOUT moving forward. Sometimes the struggles we face are simply so overwhelming that it takes all the strength we have merely to hold on.

George Lacy was working as a public school teacher when he and his wife, Minnie, decided to take their vocational skills to the mission field. In 1903, the couple and their five children journeyed to Saltillo, Mexico, to organize and operate a school for girls, the Madero Institute.

Joy turned to sorrow in December 1904, when a daughter fell ill with scarlet fever. She died so quickly doctors weren't able to diagnose her illness. Shortly after that, a son also died. Not knowing what was wrong but desperate to escape the illness, Mrs. Lacy and the three oldest children boarded a train to return to Arkansas while Mr. Lacy buried their two youngest children, his heart breaking. Before the train reached home, the three remaining children also died of the fever. Lacy's letters to the foreign mission board describe in terrible simplicity the utter despair he and his wife felt in those hours. He writes these words: "Sometimes it seems more than we can bear."

Some of you are facing just such a time right now. The pain of the loss of a loved one; the struggles of caring for elderly parents who no longer remember you; the uncertainty and fears of grave illness; the loss of a job; the debilitating and misunderstood darkness of depression—all of these and so much more are real parts of a fallen world. In these moments it often seems more than we can bear. We cry out to God with questions, sometimes even in frustration and anger. When the answers aren't apparent, it often feels like He isn't there or isn't listening.

He is there and He is not silent, though the sound of His voice may be hard to discern and the touch of His hand may not be easily felt.

These are the times when the work of the Holy Spirit goes on in you even in fits of rebellion, even in the very face of spiritual doubt. When you can no longer pray, the Holy Spirit lifts your heart's deepest prayers for you. When you cannot move forward one more step, a Trinity of compassion inhabits the place where you pause. Paul understood this when he built his list in Romans 8 of the things that cannot separate us from the love of Christ. He knew clearly what we need to remember when the pain is too great: It is not necessary for us to hold on to the love of Christ in those difficult times because He is doing the work, making certain nothing that is done to us, indeed nothing that we do ourselves, separates us from His love.

George and Minnie Lacy decided to return to Mexico, to face the place of their greatest despair. Forty-six years later, when their ministry ended there, their work left behind a trail of children whose lives were touched by the same love of Christ that sustained the couple in their deepest trials. It was not their own strength that moved them through the storm. It was the promise that Christ made: "I will never leave you nor forsake you."

He has not left you, either.

WEEK 30

Red Sox Missionaries in a Yankees World

These words, which I am commanding you today, shall be on your heart. You shall teach them diligently to your sons and shall talk of them when you sit in your house and when you walk by the way and when you lie down and when you rise up. You shall bind them as a sign on your hand and they shall be as frontals on your forehead. You shall write them on the doorposts of your house and on your gates (DEUTERONOMY 6:6–9).

I'D BETTER CONFESS, BEFORE I begin, that I'm not a Red Sox fan, even though I live in the Boston area with a wife and children who are card-carrying members of Red Sox Nation. But I grew up in Kansas City, and I will die a Royals fan.

To be sure everyone's up to speed, let me tell you a secret. People in Red Sox Nation are not big fans of the New York Yankees. And people in Yankee Land aren't big fans of the Sox. Armed with that information, you can better understand the center of New England's universe during baseball season: Fenway Park.

On commuter trains, everybody's talking Red Sox. In conference rooms before meetings start, Manny and Papa's latest exploits are dissected as intently as the company's budget projections. Grown men and women roar in their cubicles with each Red Sox win and celebrate with gusto the absence of pinstripes in prime time.

I'm not kidding! You should be here: People who have never darkened the doors of a baseball stadium talk batting averages and pitching stats like all-stars at an old-timers game. Gentle elderly women turn into purse-wielding fanatics if someone praises A-Rod or Jeter. In every corner of Red

Sox Nation, the Boston team's latest march through traditional Yankee territory—the postseason championships—dominates the landscape. Oh, to be sure, there are other baseball teams out there. I know that, and you know that, but that's because we've lived in those other places where the smack of the ball against the wood of the bat still rings sweetly in our ears. (Here in the Northeast, that smack you just heard is somebody's briefcase walloping a tourist wearing a Yankees hat on the Freedom Trail.)

In Red Sox Nation, it isn't enough to be fans; they want to make you fans, too.

Day after day, hour by hour, men and women—*even those whose whole lives usually begin and end with their careers*—set aside their vocational passions to pursue their love for the Sox. They sleep Sox, eat Sox, and wear out the ears of anyone daring to declare themselves unconverted, undecided, or worse—pro-Yankees. Meek and quiet on most days, their voices roar with unity around September and October. Without fear, without restraint, without embarrassment, without even a hint of reluctance, they talk about something very important to them: Red Sox baseball!

There's no timidity here. Red Sox lingo fills the air, permeating the lives and language of the true believers. Zealous and passionate, they are missionaries for the Splendid Splinter (also known as Ted Williams), Yastremski, Manny Ramirez, and Jason Varitek.

If only we workplace Christians could get as excited about the gospel!

In New England, the team you root for is not considered a private matter. *Neither is Jesus.*

WEEK 31

Prayers for the Workplace

"Pray without ceasing" (THE APOSTLE PAUL in 1 THESSALONIANS 5:17).

HERE ARE SOME WAYS TO think about prayer for the people God places around us on the job:

1. Pray over our calendars. Asking God at the beginning of our workday to be with us in our contacts helps us discover ways to show those that we interact with the character of God. As we pray for our interactions with our contacts, one of the fringe benefits might be fewer incidents of inappropriate behavior toward them. When we pray for others, we experience the amazing effect of not feeling animosity toward them, and when we actually see those people we have been praying for, we are reminded of our prayers on their behalf. This reminder makes us conscious of their need for Christ (if they aren't Christians) or their need to be strengthened and encouraged (if they are followers of Christ).

2. Pray for those we manage or lead. Scripture defines work as one of the ways we serve God, and this means the people we manage have been placed there not only as corporate responsibilities but as spiritual ones as well. We must pray for God's wisdom in dealing with them, reflecting the character of God in our management styles.

3. Pray for those who manage or lead us. While our managers have responsibility for us, we as Christians have an obligation to pray for those in authority over us. Praying for our managers reminds us of their humanity and of their need for Christ. Often our hearts will be softened, enabling us to reflect the character of God even in

those times when we might face unreasonable demands or unfair treatment.

4. Pray for God to make it clear whom He wants us to talk to about Him that day and who might benefit from our silence about matters of faith in that moment. God does not play head games with us. When we seek His direction, His will becomes clear to us, and this includes even the discussions we have about Him on the job.

5. Divide up the names of the people we pray for, and assign them to certain days of the week. Because of often insanely hectic paces, the number of people we can effectively, individually pray for is limited. Consider praying for a different list of people each day. While that list will often change based on your calendar, we've discovered this regular pattern of prayer for coworkers and others often makes us better able to respond like Christ during unexpected encounters with them, including times of conflict.

The work of evangelism is primarily the work of the Holy Spirit, but it is our work as well. Just as the Holy Spirit softens hearts, including our own, so too does prayer change the way we see those who need to hear about the One who offers grace that lasts forever.

WEEK 32

Why Do You Work?

Whatever you do, work at it with all your heart, as working for the Lord, not for men, since you know that you will receive an inheritance from the Lord as a reward. It is the Lord Christ you are serving (COLOSSIANS 3:23–24 NIV).

WHY THE *SPECIFIC KIND* OF work you do? Why the *place* you're working now?

Do those questions matter?

In the world we have created in our heads, there are no right answers to these questions. If you aren't a follower of Jesus Christ or if you don't accept the Bible as the final authority on matters of faith and practice, then you're living in that world where there are no (or few) right or wrong answers. But working followers of Jesus Christ who accept Scripture as authoritative don't have the luxury of living in that make-believe world.

We work because God said so (Genesis 1:26–29; 2:15; and, less glamorously after the fall, Genesis 3:17–19). When He made us, He placed in us a nature that is restless without work and that is incomplete without something meaningful to do. If we don't work, we don't satisfy the deepest longing of our soul, and we certainly don't please God (Colossians 3:23–24; 1 Thessalonians 5:12–13; 2 Thessalonians 3:6–14). Many think work is a villain, that it produces stress that makes life hard. It isn't work that's the culprit but rather the impact sin has on work. (See Genesis 3:17–19 again.)

So if we're supposed to work because God told us to, then what *kind of work? This* is where most of us get tripped up. We make one of three mistakes: (1) we let life and the river of circumstance determine what we do for work[1]; or (2) we choose the kind of work that serves *us* best; or (3) we wait around for a magic spiritual moment when God reveals His special will for our lives.

Once we've discovered that we work because God said so, it's surprising to discover we get to *choose* how we want to work. But we do! But, there *is* a catch. Because we're followers of Jesus and because we're called to imitate Him, we're supposed to choose work that serves others, not us (Philippians 2:1–11). That doesn't mean it can't be fun or that it won't have its rewards, but it does mean if we pick it *because* it's fun or it has its rewards, we've already stepped off the narrow path to godly contentedness. Followers of Jesus Christ are to live their lives in service and sacrifice to others (Romans 12:1–2; Galatians 2:20; Philippians 1:21). Freedom in Christ means we are free to choose work that serves others. It's also an intentional process, meaning we can't just "let go and let God," drifting along aimlessly wherever the river of circumstance carries us. (Note to drifters: There's a waterfall ahead.)

By the time we get to the third question (Why this place?), we should already understand that the people we serve in a particular place matter to God. Who we work with and who is impacted by our work are not merely economic considerations; these issues are part of our spiritual service. Work is not merely a means to an end or a place to put in time or raise funds. Our workplace *can be* holy ground.

When we discover we work because God wants us to work, then even difficult work—or difficult times at work—become faithful service to the Father. This realization strengthens our ability to tolerate work when it seems intolerable. Merely battling through the Sunday-night blues and Monday-morning alarm clock to make it to our cubicles or cabs becomes a triumph of obedience that honors God.

Discovering we have freedom to choose where we obey God—and discovering God wants us to hand that freedom back to Him by serving others—enables us to discover the key to truly meaningful endeavor.

We've also said, in the most powerful way we humans are able, that we love God.

---

1. We want to acknowledge not all people are free to choose their work. God is still honored when we choose to do our jobs as though we work directly for Him, even when those jobs are thrust on us by circumstances beyond our control and even when those circumstances are difficult.

WEEK 33

The Damage of a Hectic Pace

Therefore be careful how you walk, not as unwise men but as wise, making the most of your time, because the days are evil. So then do not be foolish, but understand what the will of the Lord is (EPHESIANS 5:15–17).

WE CHRISTIANS LOVE THE TERM *tentmaker*. It's been a part of our vocabulary for as long as we can remember, describing men and women (often missionaries) who engage in a profession to support themselves while they share the gospel of Jesus Christ. The apostle Paul was a tentmaker, literally and figuratively. So are we.

Makers of the bags tents are stored in, however, are quite a different matter! I promise you these people drive Volkswagen Beetles, live in studio apartments, and read only *Reader's Digest* Condensed Books. They're probably the fiendish minds who created Spandex also. If it's too small, they're behind it. Try to roll a tent back up small enough to get it in one of those bags, and you'll realize exactly what I'm talking about.

All too often, our spiritual lives feel like that tent and tent-bag. While we may start our day earnestly hoping we can be faithful to the Lord, frequently the stuff of life crams itself down our throats, and we fail Him more than we honor Him. Then, late at night, when the careening, chaotic paths of work and relationships relinquish their grips on our conscious actions, our thoughts turn back to God. It can be utterly discouraging in those moments to realize how little we've thought of Him in the course of the day.

Then maybe sometime during the week we finally find time to read His Word, and we are ever more astonished at just how holy He demands us to be and how utterly unfit for His service we are indeed. How can we possibly fit this tent of unfaithfulness into the tent-bag of His call on our life?

One of the enemies of faithfulness is pace. Sometimes others—as in tyrannical bosses, small children, extraordinary circumstances, or the consequences of wrong choices—dictate pace to us. Often, though, the reckless pace of our lives is our own fault, as we chase after the windmill of plenty, prosperity, security, power, or a place of significance. A relentless pace condemns us to focus on the moment, leaving little time for earthly, tangible relationships, let alone God. If the goal of our time management system is designed to cram more accomplishment into our day, then our focus is on tasks and not on the relationship that gives meaning to those tasks.

We must each look to the pace in our lives and govern it prudently. It strengthens not only our relationship with God but with all those God has given us: family, friends, and coworkers.

We cannot think of God in the shorter journeys of our life if we fail to consider His place in the longer journeys. Planning those longer journeys—like "Where is God working and what's my place in His wall?" and "What do my children need to know about God?" and "Am I ready to give an answer when my coworker asks me the hard questions of faith?"—requires the preparation done in quiet moments that refuse to yield to the world's demand for activity.

Our tents of unfaithfulness will always be bigger than the tent-bag of holiness. Even as we recognize our continuing unworthiness, though, we must never stop yielding ourselves to obedience. The irony of "more fruit for the kingdom" is often that it demands we be less busy.

WEEK 34

Separation Canyon

For a righteous man falls seven times, and rises again, but the wicked stumble in time of calamity (PROVERBS 24:16).

IF THEY'D JUST WAITED ONE *more day!*

William Dunn, Captain O. G. Howland, and his brother Seneca were fed up. For ninety days in 1869 they fought the Colorado River with the John Wesley Powell expedition, exploring and charting the river that forged the heart of the Grand Canyon. At first the excitement of the journey was enough to motivate the trio to stick out the trials, but day-by-day their enthusiasm waned.

They were tired of the unexpected rapids—boulder-strewn spots in the river where their tranquil float became a life-threatening dash. Steering was useless, as the river had its own course charted; boats in that spot would go where the river wanted them to, regardless of how the riders felt. The members of the expedition were also fed up with the frequent portages, places where they couldn't float but instead had to carry the boats and supplies overland themselves.

In August, after nearly three months of exploration fraught with numerous disasters, the expedition faced what looked to be the toughest rapids yet, and the canyon walls were so steep, even portage wasn't an option. They would have to shoot those rapids or abandon the trek. *Enough was enough*, the elder Howland decided, and on August 28 he took his younger brother and William Dunn and hiked out of the canyon. The story goes that the younger Howland pleaded to stay, but the elder brother would have none of it.

Powell and the rest of the expedition climbed back into the boats and in minutes were through the rapids to safety. Less than a day later, they emerged from the Grand Canyon triumphant.

If only the three had waited through one more trial!

Shortly after leaving the canyon, the Howlands and Dunn were killed, some say by religious zealots in Mormon country, others say by Indians mistaking them for another trio of criminals.

History records with sad perspective this tragic turn of events, always with the same words: *just one more day.*

Surely there are days when our work lives feel like that first expedition up the canyon. The thrill of the tasks at hand yield to the hard work those tasks demand. Difficult people make the trek less pleasant than it could be, and competition often makes it less fruitful, too. The portages are too frequent, those seasons in our lives where unemployment or failure make us pack our stuff and hike through deserts to the next available place to lay in our boats. We're so busy doing the urgent that the really important slips on downstream ahead of us. We wonder how our work could matter to God when we feel like it doesn't matter to us.

It's the moments when the workplace journey isn't fun that separate the faithful from the flighty. God doesn't want us hiking out of the canyons to find some softer place to serve Him. He wants us to serve right where we are, right now—accountants and laborers, tax collectors and customer service reps, and even (just to pay the bills) programmers-turned-pizza-delivery-guys. God expects us to trust Him in the hard days like we praise Him in the fun ones, not just because it's good for us but because it's good for those around us who are watching to see if our faith really means something at crunch time.

We have an advantage the trio with Powell didn't. We know how the story ends. Even if this life is eighty years of misery, the next eighty billion years are marked by unmarred, tranquil, joyful moments with God. Fixing our eyes on how the story ends is sometimes the only way to get through the portages and rapids. It's also sometimes the only way people watching us learn about faith.

The place where the Howlands left the party is now called Separation Canyon, a haunting name for something so close to a happy ending. May God give us grace to wade through one more portage or shoot one more rapids, knowing other eyes and other people's end-tales rest on what they see us do.

WEEK 35

Nothing But Net

Simon Peter said to them, "I am going fishing." They said to him, "We will also come with you." They went out and got into the boat; and that night they caught nothing. But when the day was now breaking, Jesus stood on the beach; yet the disciples did not know that it was Jesus. So Jesus said to them, "Children, you do not have any fish, do you?" They answered Him, "No." And He said to them, "Cast the net on the right-hand side of the boat and you will find a catch." So they cast, and then they were not able to haul it in because of the great number of fish. Therefore that disciple whom Jesus loved [John] said to Peter, "It is the Lord." So when Simon Peter heard that it was the Lord, he put his outer garment on (for he was stripped for work), and threw himself into the sea (JOHN 21:3–7).

IT WAS AFTER THE RESURRECTION, and Jesus had already appeared to the disciples and others. Now a group of seven disciples were by the Sea of Tiberias. This passage from John 21 records what happened next.

At the Sea of Tiberias, Peter and the other six disciples were obviously waiting for the "What's next?" in their lives. Not content, however, to merely wait, Peter goes back to the skills that Christ had called him away from a few years before. "I am going fishing," he says.

So many times we Christians wrestle to find great things to do for God. We fail to recognize the truth that God most often comes to us while we're doing the routine things in life. This is particularly true for men and women who meet Christ during adulthood or for those of us who see our childhood belief spring to new life. Our newfound zeal presses us eagerly forward in a search to express our joy and gratitude for the work of Christ in our lives. Sometimes this causes us to abandon our commitment to the details of our lives as we seek to do big things for God. Better to imitate the disciples here at Tiberias. Joyful at the news of the resurrected Christ, bewildered perhaps by what it meant for them individually, they waited for direction rather than rushing forward on their own. And while waiting, they went back to work doing what they were skilled at doing.

Now wouldn't it be marvelous for our work/faith devotional here if the Bible recorded that the disciples were wildly successful at their job during this period of waiting? Wouldn't it fit neatly into our message to describe how God blessed their work while they waited? Instead, the Bible records their efforts produced nothing but net—no fish, no return on their invested effort.

Sometimes the work of our hands will not bring us success. Sometimes even in faithful service, even in the earnest desire to honor God with our labors, we may still fail. It is in those moments that it's most important to remember it isn't the actions or the results that most bring glory to God but the condition of our hearts. A desire to serve God glorifies Him, even when there's no visible evidence of results.

Even failure brings Him glory when our heart's desire in the effort has been faithfulness to Him. Even empty nets can be used by God to reveal Himself more fully to us or to others around us. We serve a Savior who loves us enough to reveal Himself to us in the wake of lost jobs, difficult bosses, and hard-fought fruits wherever we labor.

Courage, then, must be our watchword. Courage, perseverance, and confidence in the risen Lord.

WEEK 36

The Only Port That Matters

Others went out on the sea in ships; they were merchants on the mighty waters. They saw the works of the LORD, his wonderful deeds in the deep. For he spoke and stirred up a tempest that lifted high the waves. They mounted up to the heavens and went down to the depths; in their peril their courage melted away. They reeled and staggered like drunken men; they were at their wits' end. Then they cried out to the LORD in their trouble, and he brought them out of their distress. He stilled the storm to a whisper; the waves of the sea were hushed. They were glad when it grew calm, and he guided them to their desired haven (PSALM 107:23–30 NIV).

ONE OF THE GREAT IRONIES of our faith is that we see God most clearly during storms and trials.

It's a rare thing, indeed, when a soul is added to the kingdom of God in prosperity or peace. Humans demonstrate a remarkable penchant for ignoring God in prosperity or forgetting God when things go well. The roller-coaster faith of Israel, described most vividly in the book of Judges, teaches this truth: God's people turn their heads from Him when life gets cushy.

How ironic that truth seems to Christians! Most of us found a peace we never dreamed possible in those early moments of salvation, when— face to face with our sinful nature—we cried out to God and received in return the righteousness of Jesus. How majestic were those days when we understood God's pledge to move our sins "as far as the East is from the West" and then, just to stamp in our hearts His unending capacity to love, He went on to promise He would "remember them no more" (Psalm 103:12).

Characteristic of our human frailty, we expect that peace to last.

After all, who could believe that moment would dissipate? Who could imagine a time when we'd forget the dreadful judgment we escaped or the wondrous relief we felt at having guilt and shame lifted from our shoulders?

And yet—who among us hasn't been seduced by life's glitzy side or wearied by its struggles? Who among us hasn't longed for freedom from conflict or wished for safety and security and stress-free living? Who among us hasn't found the Spirit's call to sacrifice and service silenced by the comfort of prosperity?

This explains why evangelism is so hard in American workplaces, why the more highly developed nations struggle with and rebel against Christianity even as revival sweeps through poor and oppressed people groups. People look to themselves when things are going well; they look to God when they aren't.

Just as God works in and through the storms of life, so, too, must we. For those are the moments when others will see God most clearly; those are the moments when we're most likely to reach them for Him. Those are the moments where most of our resources, most of our energy, most of our efforts should be directed. That's when their rudderless souls will be guided to the only port that matters, the desired haven that is the great love of God.

"Whoever is wise, let him heed these things and consider the great love of the LORD" (Psalm 107:43 NIV).

WEEK 37

Best Practices

In the beginning was the Word, and the Word was with God, and the Word was God. He was in the beginning with God. All things came into being through Him, and apart from Him nothing came into being that has come into being. In Him was life, and the life was the Light of men. The Light shines in the darkness, and the darkness did not comprehend it (JOHN 1:1–5).

WHAT WORKS IN THE WORLD may not be what pleases God. We'll come back to that thought in a minute.

There's a temptation in every culture to make "best practices" the bible of that society. Because something works, or appears to work, we deem it inherently valuable and determine to replicate it. Nowhere is this more likely to occur than the workplace.

On the surface, the idea of gathering together in one place the things that work best makes sense, especially when those best practices are backed up by empirical evidence of their effectiveness. Sharing ideas that work saves time and effort, saving us from "re-inventing the wheel."

But there are dangers to "best practices," too.

For one, there's a danger that "best practices" will organize themselves into one-size-fits-all formulas. For example, in Jim Collins's bestseller *Good to Great,* he and his team of researchers developed an impressive empirical mechanism to determine what made some companies excel where others in similar circumstances were less effective. In order to do this, of course, they first had to determine a definition of *great.* Eventually they settled on cumulative stock returns as a measure of greatness and then built their project around that. For companies who view cumulative stock returns as a primary benchmark for success, the "best practices" discovered by Collins's team are useful indeed.

But what if that isn't your company's mission? What if a company exists primarily to serve a specific niche or need in society? What if a company exists primarily to provide work to hard-to-employ individuals? Are the best practices from companies whose priority is cumulative stock return the best practices for that firm? (To his credit, Collins and his team recognized this, too, and have recently released a monograph for not-for-profits.)

"Best practices" must be carefully examined, because they may shift our outcomes or our focus away from our original objectives.

Christians in the marketplace need to be especially alert to such a diversion. What works in the world may not be what pleases God. That's a hard pill to swallow, so let's set it apart for special emphasis.

What works in the world may not be what pleases God.

Too often we live our working lives in trial-and-error mode, trying to discover the right fit or the right goal or even the right job. To save ourselves time, we look around us for "best practices," people or ideas (or books) that help us find shortcuts to success in life. Unfortunately, most of those people or ideas or books define success differently from how God defines it. Still, the "best practices" often work, so we put them in play in our working lives.

It's a process that leads to immense spiritual frustration. Even when we're successful on the world's terms, we feel the tug of eternal benchmarks.

There's only one way to know if your work matters to God. There's only one way to know if the best practices of the world work in the eyes of God. There's only one way to know if what works in the world pleases God.

Every workplace action must be measured against the principles of our faith as expressed in the Bible. Every corporate goal, every personal job change, every policy and procedure must be measured against the only set of principles that won't ever change.

Those who would lead in the world must know that Word, or else they've surrendered their authority. Those who would serve Christ in tangible ways must know that Word, or else they've surrendered their effectiveness and possibly even the value of their labor.

In the beginning was the Word, and none of us who seek to make our work effective may do so without making it the central document in our existence.

WEEK 38

Points to Ponder

You are the salt of the earth; but if the salt has become tasteless, how can it be made salty again? It is no longer good for anything, except to be thrown out and trampled under foot by men. You are the light of the world (MATTHEW 5:13–14).

SOME WORK/FAITH THOUGHTS TO PONDER this week:

- No labor on our part makes us worthy of a relationship with God, so no career should ever so consume our being that it distracts us from God. This is as true for pastors as it is for stockbrokers or programmers.
- Survival of the fittest is not a biblical concept.
- Flattery and compromise don't glorify God, but neither do judgmental attitudes and legalistic demeanors. Competence and compassion are important characteristics for Christians who want their work to matter for God.
- We must never make faith in Jesus Christ about doing the right thing. Ethics is a by-product of faith and not a central tenet. Faith in Jesus Christ is about grace. Anything else leads people to believe faith is performance based and that it's legalistic. It also leads them to believe that good people go to heaven just by being good.
- Anything that contradicts Scripture isn't from God.
- God's silence usually means we already have enough information to make a decision.
- God not only forgives sin, He forgets it.
- God expects faithfulness—even in the face of trials.

- The key to handling difficult people, overcoming criticism, resisting the discouragement that comes from ridicule, or living tentatively in the face of threats is to have an eternal focus that comes only from constant interaction with God.
- Workers who have damaged or ruined their reputations because of incompetency or a lack of compassion should first look to repair these voids before adding evangelism to the purpose of their work.
- God could end all suffering today if He wanted to, but in doing so, He would cut some people off from their opportunity to be redeemed. Each day He waits gives others an opportunity to spend eternity with Him.
- Biblical illiteracy is inexcusable in our culture. The Bible is more readily accessible to us than at any other time in history. Our lack of knowledge is a form of rebellion that punishes us and those who rely on us.
- There are no secrets in Christianity and no secret principles waiting to be discovered by gurus. Jesus teaches us that anyone who claims Him as Savior has the key to understanding God's Word; anyone who doesn't know Christ as Savior can only view the Bible through a worldly and blurred perspective. God is the author of clarity; Satan is the author of confusion.

WEEK 39

The Source of Our Significance

But Jesus called them to Himself and said, "You know that the rulers of the Gentiles lord it over them, and their great men exercise authority over them. It is not this way among you, but whoever wishes to become great among you shall be your servant, and whoever wishes to be first among you shall be your slave; just as the Son of Man did not come to be served, but to serve, and to give His life a ransom for many" (MATTHEW 20:25–28).

MY ACTING SKILLS ARE SO majestic, so carefully crafted in communicating nuance and deep meaning, directors have often selected me to play the dead body in their productions—or sometimes a tree or the moon.

Lazarus is my hero in this niche of acting nirvana. Even though he lived in a culture that placed greater emphasis on men than women, God chose to tell us more about Mary and Martha than He did about Lazarus. In fact, Lazarus shares my claim to fame, being remembered most for a "dead-body" role.

Lazarus' part as a bit player gave him a wonderful opportunity to serve the kingdom in ways he could not have been expected to imagine.

At some point in our spiritual journey, we may become convinced we should be doing big things for God, producing fruit that's readily evident to Him (and often that's readily apparent to others). Our focus shifts from pursuit of success in the physical kingdom to significance in the spiritual realm. Or we set off in pursuit of significance in other arenas.

Make no mistake—producing spiritual fruit must indeed have an urgent claim on our lives. But when the reason we're doing so is to make others feel good about us or to make us feel good about ourselves, it ceases to be service and becomes self-gratification. Even measuring the impact of our labors should be done carefully, with humility, always guarding against claiming for ourselves credit for the work God is doing through us.

We must be willing to appear insignificant to the kingdom if we want to experience the true joy of serving that kingdom. We must be satisfied with bit roles—like Lazarus—in which our efforts are wholly dependent on God's blessing, His work, to produce fruit. God doesn't need us in order to accomplish His will, yet He gives us the opportunity to be in relationship with Him as we work where He's working. We are significant because He made us significant; we are never significant because of what we do for Him.

Don't be fooled into thinking God can't use you as you go about your daily tasks. God is as much at work in the cubicles as He is in the sanctuary. He's as interested in being in relationship with you during the labor negotiations as He is in hearing from you in your quiet time. Service in the kingdom only has rank in our eyes, from our perspective. Every action, every moment surrendered to Him out of gratitude and obedience is an opportunity for Him to work in us, and in those around us, even if we never see the effect this side of eternity.

The Westminster Catechism declares that "man's chief end is to glorify God, and enjoy Him forever." We glorify and enjoy Him best when our thoughts, our actions, and our sacrifices are focused on Him, and not on how they make us feel about ourselves.

WEEK 40

Bring On the Storms

Finally, be strong in the Lord and in his mighty power. Put on the full armor of God so that you can take your stand against the devil's schemes. For our struggle is not against flesh and blood, but against the rulers, against the authorities, against the powers of this dark world and against the spiritual forces of evil in the heavenly realms. Therefore put on the full armor of God, so that when the day of evil comes, you may be able to stand your ground, and after you have done everything, to stand. Stand firm then, with the belt of truth buckled around your waist, with the breastplate of righteousness in place, and with your feet fitted with the readiness that comes from the gospel of peace. In addition to all this, take up the shield of faith, with which you can extinguish all the flaming arrows of the evil one. Take the helmet of salvation and the sword of the Spirit, which is the word of God. And pray in the Spirit on all occasions with all kinds of prayers and requests. With this in mind, be alert and always keep on praying for all the saints (EPHESIANS 6:10–18 NIV).

SUCCESSFUL PEOPLE, BY AND LARGE, aren't interested in God until a crisis hits their life. With money in the bank and careers on course, few people will slow down long enough to tackle questions of eternity. For the most part, they turn to God or to people who they think may know Him only when situations become stormy.

If we don't know Him before we get rich, chances aren't good we'll ever meet Him. That's why Jesus said camels will pass through needles more easily than rich people will slip through the gates of heaven. It isn't that being rich is wrong; it's that being rich draws us away from awareness that we need God.

In fact, being poor can be just as dangerous, especially if trying to get rich is our answer to being poor, or if we're so focused on what other people have that we don't have that we yearn our days away.

Anything that distracts us from complete dependence on God becomes an immensely destructive force in our life. *In today's culture, the biggest culprit is work.* In a total reversal of what God intended, we've managed to make work the place where we're least aware of God. Genesis teaches us work was intended to put us in touch with Him.

So should we revert to sackcloth and ashes? Head off to a monastery and spend our days in quiet contemplation?

Not likely. God is an active God, and—*made in His image*—we're to be an active people.

But we must guard our hearts. The apostle Paul describes it as being in the world without being like the world. Life isn't lived only in churches; it's also lived in offices and jobsites and homes and concert halls and classrooms and every other place where activity occurs. We're to be in those places doing the things others do in those places. Unlike others, though, we're to be doing them for God, in the narrow way He intends them to be done. The moment we switch to doing work for ourselves or break God's commands in the ways we do it, we've lost touch with God.

Then we look and feel and act like the people who don't know Him, and, tragically, we make it even harder for them to see Him in and through us.

As hard as this is to hear (and say), if it's the storms in life that keep us close to God, then Lord, *bring on the storms.*

We can't make it on our own.

WEEK 41

Unemployment's Spiritual Challenges

I pray that out of his glorious riches he may strengthen you with power through his Spirit in your inner being, so that Christ may dwell in your hearts through faith. And I pray that you, being rooted and established in love, may have power, together with all the saints, to grasp how wide and long and high and deep is the love of Christ, and to know this love that surpasses knowledge—that you may be filled to the measure of all the fullness of God (EPHESIANS 3:16–19 NIV).

MONTE'S PHONE SELDOM RINGS ANYMORE. *Seven months of unemployment have wrung all the words out of his well-meaning friends, and they no longer know what to say to encourage him. Dozens of resumes and a handful of interviews have produced only rejection, and Monte's once-certain confidence is now disappearing. He feels alone, uncertain, and scared this time might never end.*

Unemployment is seldom easy. In fact, for a working follower of Jesus Christ, it often presents not only a fiscal crisis but a spiritual crisis as well. *"Where is God in this job search,"* we wonder, *"and why is this happening to me?"* The longer the unemployment lasts or the more rejections we receive or the tighter the finances get, the more difficult the struggle becomes at all levels.

How should we respond in these moments?

Most of us know the advice for trying to find work. Good resumes; effective networking; continuous, confident pursuit. Bookstores, friends in business, human resource professionals, and even job-search firms are often able to help us with the practical aspects of the job search.

Where do we turn, though, to face the emotional and spiritual trials of unemployment?

First, we must recognize the dangers this time presents. Joblessness attacks our confidence and self-esteem; it may isolate us, and it presents the temptation for us to isolate ourselves further. It may be embarrassing, and it can trigger our worst behaviors, causing us to lash out at those around us. It can also present practical challenges, such as not having enough money to pay the bills or even to buy groceries. It may cause us to doubt God's involvement or interest in our daily lives—in some instances, even cause us to doubt His very existence.

Countering these dangers requires concentrated planning at the outset of unemployment. To fight the isolation, gather a circle of friends you know cares deeply about you and ask them to pray with you and for you. In most cases, you shouldn't make this the group helping you get a job. These are your prayer warriors, the people who reinforce your value apart from the results of your job search.

Consider setting aside a block of time each week of your unemployment to spend extra time in prayer and Bible study. Sometimes you are out of work because God wants your attention. But even in those times when being out of work has nothing to do with your spiritual state, setting aside extra hours in this forced sabbatical can calm your soul and produce unexpected spiritual growth in the midst of struggle.

We are not immune from falling or failing, but we do have a resource in the heavenly Father, One who promises never to leave us or forsake us. Failing to call upon Him honestly and earnestly denies us access to His comforting presence in the midst of the time we need Him most.

WEEK 42

The Other Side of Why

For though we live in the world, we do not wage war as the world does. The weapons we fight with are not the weapons of the world. On the contrary, they have divine power to demolish strongholds. We demolish arguments and every pretension that sets itself up against the knowledge of God, and we take captive every thought to make it obedient to Christ. And we will be ready to punish every act of disobedience, once your obedience is complete (2 CORINTHIANS 10:3–6 NIV).

FOR CENTURIES CHRISTIANS LIVED WITH the misguided notion that only people who worked for the church were doing God's work. This led to two-tiered thinking about people and jobs: Missionaries and pastors were considered to be doing really important work, while the rest of us were merely making the money necessary to fund missionaries and pastors doing the really important work.

While Martin Luther and the great leaders of the Protestant Reformation of the 1500s realized that all work is God's work, their teachings didn't really take hold until sometime in the twentieth century when this wrong-headed thinking took a much-needed hit and people began to rediscover God really values other work, too. It should have been good news for Christians and good news for the world.

Quite frankly, it should have pushed back the darkness. If twelve disciples drawn from both blue-collar (fishing) and white-collar (tax collecting) fields could re-shape the Old World, imagine what thousands, even millions, of workers could do today!

It isn't working that way, is it?

Why not?

Perhaps it's because we've turned the workplace back into a journey of self-discovery and self-fulfillment instead of the place for sacrifice and service. There's no better way to turn a God thing into a good thing, and in the kingdom economy, good is never enough.

Here are five things to think about as we serve God at work this week:

1. The reason those twelve workers changed their world is because they first had the chance to know and spend time with Jesus. Too many of us are charging out into the world to do good without knowing God well enough. That leaves us doing what seems right in our own eyes instead of operating with the wisdom of the Father.

2. If we want our work to matter to God, then the primary reason we're doing it has to be for something other than serving self. Complete this sentence: I work because _____. Ask God to make your answer about Him and about others, if it isn't already. Especially in Western culture, too many of us are in the workplace to get something for ourselves instead of to give something of ourselves to it.

3. Busyness is replacing love of money as the prime enemy of Christians. While greed still rocks the culture, lots of people who love God are making it past the first hurdles of selfishness and gluttony, only to stumble over isolation from God. The reason we were created is to be in relationship with God. When our calendars cut us off from Him, His Word, and His church, everything else suffers.

4. The world desperately needs us. Like every other corner of creation, the workplace needs the redemptive presence of men and women redeemed by Christ.

5. Nothing is impossible for God. Just as He blesses the efforts of pastors and missionaries in their work, so too will He bless the efforts of laborers everywhere else.

Imagine a world filled with Christians seeing themselves as missionaries to their workplaces; shepherds to their professions; and ambassadors of truth and light.

Imagine what 12 x 12 x 12 x 12 x Jesus could accomplish.

WEEK 43

Let Me See the Chariots

When the servant of the man of God got up and went out early the next morning, an army with horses and chariots had surrounded the city. "Oh, my lord, what shall we do?" the servant asked. "Don't be afraid," the prophet answered. "Those who are with us are more than those who are with them." And Elisha prayed, "O LORD, open his eyes so he may see." Then the LORD opened the servant's eyes, and he looked and saw the hills full of horses and chariots of fire all around Elisha (2 KINGS 6:15–17 NIV).

"WHAT DO YOU DO FOR a living?" the middle-seat passenger asked.

You really should see how many people flinch when I tell them I'm a workplace chaplain. I suspect they're afraid I'm about to browbeat them for Jesus. Usually, though, they just can't help themselves. Because they've never heard of workplace chaplains, curiosity gets the better of them, and we almost always settle into an enlightening discussion.

On this particular flight, this particular passenger discovered he was sandwiched in between *two* Christians, so I'm pretty sure he was praying to a god he didn't know to put us both to sleep—which, of course, didn't happen.

Gradually, the three of us warmed to each other, and we ended up talking about whether God pays attention to our work. My fellow Christian in the window seat had an optimistic answer, pointing to the progress in technology and the advances in medicine and the creation of tools that made life easier. These, he assured us, were evidence things were getting better and better as humans understood more about life and more about God.

Our non-Christian seatmate took quite the opposite view, and he seemed genuinely offended at the optimism just expressed. Picking up his newspaper, he moved through the national news and then the business sections and finally even to the local section pointing to story after story after story that argued against the "better-world" theory. Then he dropped his voice and whispered to us quietly, "I frankly think your God is losing."

I thought about his answer carefully. I marveled at how close to the truth—and how far from the truth—he was in his reply.

While the media pummels us with evidence of the dark and seamy sides of life, it's the brokenness behind the façade of busy working faces that tells the story even more poignantly. Workers aren't just workers. They are husbands with distant wives, parents with distant children, children with ailing parents. They're struggling to pay bills, rescue the mortgage, and find health care. Some are lonely, many are depressed, and more than a few are convinced God isn't even interested in the battles they're fighting.

So yes, this world with its sin-stained side effects is finding old ways to make new cultures squirm. And yes, the struggle can sometimes make even longtime Christians wonder if we aren't outgunned and outmaneuvered.

That's when we must ask God to show us the chariots of fire. We struggle not, the apostle Paul says, with "flesh and blood, but against the rulers, against the authorities, against the powers of this dark world and against the spiritual forces of evil in the heavenly realms" (Ephesians 6:12 NIV).

For a time, God holds His power and judgment in check, pulling His punches in mercy, while Satan taunts Him and His creation with evil and its influence. That's when we're tempted to take our eyes off our Savior, and we're easily persuaded things are good enough, or, conversely, that things are just too bad, too dark, too hopeless. That's when we must look to the hills and see the chariots of fire in the story of Elisha, reminding us we serve the King of Kings and Lord of Lords, who loved us so much He suffered our fate to free us from despair and destruction.

Only then will false optimism be replaced by real hope, found in service to the only reality that isn't bound by time and space. Only then will we remember, *"Those who are with us are more than those who are with them."*

WEEK 44

One More Year

And [Jesus] began telling this parable: "A man had a fig tree which had been planted in his vineyard; and he came looking for fruit on it and did not find any. And he said to the vineyard-keeper, 'Behold, for three years I have come looking for fruit on this fig tree without finding any. Cut it down! Why does it even use up the ground?' And [the vineyard-keeper] answered and said to him, 'Let it alone, sir, for this year too, until I dig around it and put in fertilizer; and if it bears fruit next year, fine; but if not, cut it down'" (LUKE 13:6–9).

HANS EGEDE SET SAIL FOR Greenland in 1721 full of passion and adventure. Like many missionaries before him, his zeal for spreading the gospel outpaced his preparation. He had little idea of the obstacles he would face. For nearly twelve years his mission made little progress, hampered in a huge way by difficulty mastering the tongue of the Inuits, the Eskimos inhabiting the land. Egede also suffered from another malady, one not altogether uncommon among present-day Christians: a stern demeanor that played out as impatience with the very people he sought to serve. Without any apparent evidence of compassion and at a linguistic loss to express even the fundamental principle—the love of Christ—in the language of the Inuit, Egede's mission seemed doomed to failure. Indeed, in 1730 the king actually recalled the mission to Denmark.

Egede remained behind, begging for more time to break the frozen hearts of the icy land, perhaps *still* not fully realizing his own heart had not yet melted.

In 1733, a smallpox epidemic swept through the area, wiping out nearly two-thirds of the native population. It was an epidemic carried to the Inuits by Egede's own mission, and it would eventually claim Egede's wife as well. Grieving the loss of his wife and stunned by the enormous realization of his own role in spreading this disease, the missionary's heart melted. In truly heroic fashion, he ministered to the sick and dying, unlocking in his brokenness what had previously been a stone wall of reception to the gospel message.

Imagine the courage it took to face the horrors of an epidemic he had at least partially caused; imagine the guilt he had to overcome as he realized how long it had taken him to find the compassion of Christ in his own heart! "Give me more time," he begged the Danish king; but it was the King of Kings whose love would turn the tide—only after it had changed the heart of Egede himself.

The "hard soil" around the "fig trees" in our workplace and our culture may be hard because it hasn't been softened by our own exercise of the compassion of Christ. The "hard soil" may well be us, too busy living to learn to love, too busy being self-absorbed to realize the gap between Jesus and our coworkers is our own lack of compassion, our own lack of urgency.

Like Hans Egede, we sometimes find ourselves railing against the very people God sends us to serve, frustrated by our inability to get them to see things our way or blinded by our own agendas. Maybe, in fact, it is our own hearts that need melting.

The language of our faith is disappearing from our culture, rapidly replaced by an impenetrable wall of rules and expectations. We increasingly find ourselves struggling to express the gospel in terms our colleagues, coworkers, friends, and family can comprehend.

Worse, the essence of our faith may be hiding from *us*, as we obscure the love of Christ behind a stern impatience—even righteous indignation—that causes us to see the people God places in our paths as adversaries instead of people in need of a Savior.

We should be pleading with God to melt our hearts and to teach us to love our enemies and our friends, for surely the love of Christ is most attractive when it shows itself in us.

WEEK 45

The Lord's Commission

How, then, can they call on the one they have not believed in? And how can they believe in the one of whom they have not heard? And how can they hear without someone preaching to them? And how can they preach unless they are sent? As it is written, "How beautiful are the feet of those who bring good news!" (ROMANS 10:14–15 NIV).

THE BODY OF CHRIST HAS never relied on you more than it does right now, and not because it needs your tithe. In fact, rarely in American history has the work of the church been more reliant on the workplaces of its members. And not for dollars, either.

The need is so great, it may finally be time to consider commissioning mechanics the way we once commissioned missionaries headed overseas.

Why?

More and more people are actively distancing themselves from the places where they're likely to hear about God. An increasing number of people are choosing *not* to attend worship services, and even those who do attend Sunday services aren't likely to find themselves in Sunday school or Bible studies, where a deeper word is taught and heard. Entire generations are being raised without encountering the Bible. Even among the faithful, biblical illiteracy is reaching epidemic levels.

So while the local church remains the most important human institution in the body of Christ, people are more likely to see and hear about God in our working lives than in our church lives. While our jobs have always mattered to God, there's a heightened urgency to the mission of our working selves in this culture. People who have no faith look to us to break down what they call the "impenetrable language of faith."

Just as missionaries once carried the gospel to other lands and translated the truths of Scripture into those foreign languages, now we too must be missionaries to our workplaces, where we find growing numbers of people intellectually distant from God. In the vernacular of historic Christianity, we must "Wycliffe the workplace."

This is in stark contrast to America's early history, when the church played a pivotal role in the social, educational, and political life of nearly every citizen. [1]

Once, faith was embedded in our culture[2] and pastors' voices echoed into every corner of life because the people who populated those corners were sitting in their pews. While the pastor's role remains as important as ever, now it is the workday Christian whose voice must ring out first in places where the pastor's voice will never reach.

So Paul's words beckon to us with special significance in this hour, charging us as mechanics and doctors and programmers and truck drivers and politicians and stay-at-home moms to be the "beautiful feet" that answer the query, "How can they know?"

Do not be found lacking when the King asks, "Who will bear my message?" His commission rests on you. And me.

---

1. In fact, in the hundred plus years before the American Civil War, the body of Christ in general, and the clergy in particular, controlled the educational institutions of the United States. They also had a powerful hold on the teaching and writing of political and economic theory. Of the 288 college presidents in the United States just before the Civil War, 262 were ordained ministers. Of these 262, 156 were strict Calvinistic Protestants, 30 were Baptist, and 28 were Methodist. In mid-nineteenth-century America, it was almost exclusively pastors who wrote political and economic textbooks. Baptist pastor Frances Wayland, longtime president of Brown University, wrote the leading economic and political textbook, *The Elements of Political Economy,* and it remained the preferred text/theory in American colleges and universities for almost fifty years, through the 1870s.

2. Benjamin Franklin could write about an obscure Old Testament character, and everyone in America knew what he meant because the Bible was both a spiritual guide *and* a school textbook used to teach reading

WEEK 46

The Best Argument

His parents said this because they were afraid of the Jews; for the Jews had already agreed that if anyone confessed Him to be Christ, he was to be put out of the synagogue. For this reason his parents said, "He is of age; ask him." So a second time they called the man who had been blind, and said to him, "Give glory to God; we know that [Jesus] is a sinner." He then answered, "Whether He is a sinner, I do not know; one thing I do know, that though I was blind, now I see" (JOHN 9:22–25).

JUST THE AMBASSADOR AND I, and neither of us were happy. Of course, in my defense, I didn't know right away that he was an ambassador.

When he sat down next to me on the train, it wasn't his first choice—or mine. Eight-hour train rides are seldom fun, but they're even less enjoyable if you don't have an empty seat next to you. As courtesy dictated, we grunted our greetings to each other, made some perfunctory small talk, and then retired to our inner shells, just hoping to be left alone.

An hour into the ride, I pulled out a Bible. I heard a huge sigh. Not a mild one, mind you, but a huge one—the kind that makes people six seats away take notice. So I looked his way. "You're not going to tell me," he bellowed, "that you believe that stuff!"

That was it. Stuffy train. Crowded seats. And a sigh? The debate began.

"What stuff?" I countered. (Pretty witty, huh?)

For the better part of the next two hours, we waged verbal warfare, discovering as we did that we were both enjoying the banter more than we cared to admit. Gradually our stories merged into the debate. His was infinitely more interesting than mine. Thirty plus years in the State Department, two terms as ambassador to big countries, and now settling into teaching as part of his retirement plan. Once I heard the name I recognized it, of course, but by then we were far enough into the verbal thrust-and-parry that I was no longer in a position to be awed.

Hour three turned into something different. Slowing down over our meals, we started asking questions instead of issuing statements. I asked him how he came to do what he did. Strangely enough, he asked me how it was I came to be a "believer"—his term for Christians.

I listened to his story and asked questions. I was genuinely interested in his answers.

He listened to my story and asked questions. And more questions. And still more questions. By now I thought for sure this was going to turn into one of those tales where you sit down next to somebody and lead him to the Lord. I was writing the text in my head as I anticipated the outcome.

It didn't happen that way.

We talked without stopping until the train stopped moving, and then we exchanged business cards, promising to follow up with each other again. As he left the train, he turned to me and said, "By the way, the best part of your argument isn't what you think Jesus can do for me. It's what He's done for you."

Somehow I always seem to let that single truth slip away. The most important ingredient to living life surrendered to Christ is remembering what He's done for me. It's also the most convincing argument I'll ever have to offer as His ambassador.

WEEK 47

Eyes on the Fence Post

Brethren, I do not regard myself as having laid hold of it yet; but one thing I do: forgetting what lies behind and reaching forward to what lies ahead, I press on toward the goal for the prize of the upward call of God in Christ Jesus (PHILIPPIANS 3:13–14).

IT LOOKED LIKE THE WORK of a drunken sailor.

My first day on the tractor and, oh, the heady feeling! A crisp morning breeze brushes across the field. Crickets and country silence yield to the roar of that engine. Dropping the plow into the soil, I head out across the field. My gaze wanders over the landscape to see if anyone is watching. I look down at the gauges and gearshift, squeezing the cold steel of the steering wheel, admiring the power at my disposal. Finally, I look back to view the results.

It looks like the work of a drunken sailor!

Instead of the ramrod-straight line I expect, there's the form of a slithering snake, with more bends and curves than a NASCAR road course, a little like Watkins Glen. Somehow, I know this isn't what they mean by "amber *waves* of grain."

"Plow with your eye on the fence post." The advice offered to me over and over again rings in my ears. In my boisterous self-confidence, I'd forgotten or ignored it. Sheepishly, I start back the other way, this time with my eyes frozen on the fence post in the distance. Like an architect with a straightedge, the plow cuts a line directly across the field.

Most days, we make that same error in our jobs. We just *know* our eyes should be focused on Jesus Christ, but the distractions steal our attention. We're looking to see who's noticing us, or we're basking in the exuberance of authority. Or maybe the cares of this world are choking us even as we feign nonchalance, chugging tenaciously up the mountain of our routines. Or perhaps our eyes are distracted by unpaid bills, un-kept promises, the fear of a disappearing paycheck, or any of a hundred struggles common to our lives this side of eternity.

Regardless of our circumstances, be they joy or sorrow, doing the work of our hands and heads requires us to fix our eyes on Jesus, "the author and finisher of our faith." Only then are we able to look back on the wake of our efforts and see results that honor God. *Only then* can others look at the jobs we do and see our faith as well.

While the circumstances of our lives are often beyond our control, we *can* control where we fix our gaze. God gave us His Son to remove the barriers between us and Him, but He also gave us the Spirit to move us inexorably closer to Him, and He gave us His Word as a vital guide to understanding Him. He promises He will be found by those who seek Him.

Plow with your eye on the fence post.

WEEK 48

Your God Matters at Work

In all your ways acknowledge Him, and He will make your paths straight (PROVERBS 3:6).

EVERY CHRISTIAN IS CALLED TO full-time service for God. The places where we serve will look different, but the principles that guide us are absolute, eternal, and practical, even in places where God isn't always welcome. Here are a few ways to consider the influence your faith is having on your work and the people who surround you there.

- Why did I pick this job? Did I consult God in the decision?
- Does the product or service I produce offer value to the culture that is consistent with God's moral principles?
- Does *the way* I provide those products or services offer value to the culture that is consistent with God's moral principles?
- Is the marketing of those products and services consistent with God's moral principles?
- Does my management of the budget areas I'm responsible for reflect principles of stewardship?
- Am I making decisions that reflect concern for the long-term well-being of the investors, owners, customers, and employees where I serve?
- Are the workers, coworkers, and customers I'm responsible for being treated with dignity?
- Are the workers, coworkers, and customers I'm responsible for being treated with equity?
- Are the workers, coworkers, and customers I'm responsible for being treated with justice and, where possible, with mercy?

- Am I resolving conflict at work in ways that honor God?
- Am I differentiating between mistakes (the natural result of trial and error/research and development processes) and negligence (the unnatural result of not being diligent in labors)?
- Do I refrain from criticizing customers, coworkers, and employees to others?
- Do I exhibit forgiveness?
- Are the expectations of my job reasonable, allowing me to meet the other requirements God gives me in life?
- Are my expectations of my workers reasonable, allowing them to meet the other requirements God gives them?
- Do my memorandums, reports, conversations, discussions, and other communications reflect a commitment to honesty?
- Do I withhold information that might be useful to others in my company because it could give them an advantage in promotion or influence?
- Do my natural conversations at work reflect the nature and depth of my relationship with Jesus Christ?
- Do I refrain from retaliation against customers, coworkers, and competitors?
- Do I know my coworkers well enough to describe my faith in terms they can understand when the opportunity presents itself?
- Am I willing to sacrifice gain in my own career if it produces an outcome that serves others in my work culture more effectively?

The joy of the journey is realizing God speaks to each of us through His Word, turning timeless principles into timely insights for our own marketplace moments.

WEEK 49

The End of Empty Nets

Early in the morning, Jesus stood on the shore, but the disciples did not realize that it was Jesus. He called out to them, "Friends, haven't you any fish?" "No," they answered. He said, "Throw your net on the right side of the boat and you will find some." When they did, they were unable to haul the net in because of the large number of fish (JOHN 21:4–6 NIV).

IT WOULD BE OUR LAST time together this side of eternity, and he was *still* teaching me life lessons. "Put your hands out," he said, barely able to see me over the railing of the hospital bed. Leaning across the rail, I did as he asked. He reached up and took my hands in his, using my hands to form a cup. "This is before Jesus." Then he turned both hands over so my palms were facing down. "This is after Jesus. Stop waiting for blessings and get to work."

Message received.

It was always that simple to Francis. Anybody who didn't know Jesus needed to receive, because *nothing* they did or said mattered until they did; anybody who did know Jesus needed to work, because *everything* they did or said after that mattered.

Like it or not, it's that simple for the rest of us too.

Before Christ, our souls yearn for a link to eternity that answers the earnest beckoning for security and significance. It is natural for our hands to be cupped in anticipation and our ears to be listening for eternal messages. After Christ, however, our life is defined not by waiting and listening with palms stretched upward in seeking but in labor and fruit produced by hands turned palms down to the work at hand.

Those Christians who live their lives with their hands cupped find they are perpetually frustrated. No matter what blessings flow into those hands, it is never enough to satisfy the soul. Only when we shift our focus from what we can get to what we can do will we find the joy that transcends circumstance. Only then will we truly be one with Christ.

Jesus calls us not just to eternal life but also to companionship with Him. Those who seek to truly know Him discover quickly He is rarely idle and is never selfish. To know Christ is to share His labors—indeed, on this side of eternity, even sometimes to share His suffering.

Like Simon Peter and his friends that morning in Galilee, we will soon discover that the difference between empty nets (meaningless labor) and full nets (work and words and actions that matter into eternity) is Jesus Christ.

The days of empty nets can end now. If you've turned your heart to Jesus, then turn your hands to Him also. It will be the start of an adventure that never ends.

WEEK 50

He's Already There

What is man that You take thought of him, and the son of man that You care for him? Yet You have made him a little lower than God, and You crown him with glory and majesty! You make him to rule over the works of Your hands; You have put all things under his feet, all sheep and oxen, and also the beasts of the field, the birds of the heavens and the fish of the sea, whatever passes through the paths of the seas. O LORD, our Lord, how majestic is Your name in all the earth! (PSALM 8:4–9).

IF YOU'RE LIKE I AM, you grew up thinking heaven will be one continuous, never-ending worship service, where we all stand around in robes singing praises and hymns to God. If you're like I am, you were also afraid to appear ungrateful by admitting that those eternal festivities didn't sound like very much fun.

If you're like I am, you grew up thinking doing God's work was something pastors and evangelists did, and the rest of us worked to give them the money to do it. That, too, didn't sound like much fun.

Nothing could be further from the truth.

Made in the image of our Creator, we carry His work ethic, His creativity, His passion for excellence, His desires to love and to tend and to nurture. Here, on this earth, we tainted that image, fracturing not only its substance but its appearance by our sins and sin natures. Still, though, the image itself remains in us, a dormant majesty waiting for a signal to emerge.

That signal, of course, is our acknowledgment of Jesus Christ as Savior, an act that makes us one with Christ. While we retain our sinful bodies with their continuous tendency to rebel, our union with Christ enables us to be in fellowship with God and to be led and fed by the Holy Spirit. Now, the meatpacker's labors become as holy and honoring to God as the pastor's labors.

God is at work in every corner of creation, not just the church. He is present in the stock market and the supermarket, in the airlines and the rail lines, in the assembly line and the picket line. When we become one with Christ, we join Him where He is already at work. It makes our service in those places service to Him.

When we realize that God is working where we earn our living, where we volunteer our labors, where we tend our children or our loved ones or our neighbors, we get our first real glimpse of what heaven will be like. Rather than a huge throng of robe-laden beings singing praises, we will discover the new heaven and new earth, a place where crops will be cultivated, meals will be prepared and served, pictures will be painted, poems will be written, products will be delivered, and all of the above will be managed—but with the marvelous absence of all those dents our present work takes from our sinful natures.

When we become one with Christ, we don't suddenly carry God from our church pews to our offices or assembly lines. No, when we become one with Christ, the Holy Spirit removes the scales from our eternal eyes, enabling us to see that God has been busy in our workplace all along.

Let the Holy Spirit open our eyes to God's labors in our workplace. Despite any brokenness we may encounter, He is there and He is not silent.

WEEK 51

Who Is My Neighbor?

But he wanted to justify himself, so he [a lawyer] asked Jesus, "And who is my neighbor?" (LUKE 10:29 NIV).

WE WERE IN LINE AT the ice cream shop when I noticed him. His face bore the marks of too many bar-fights, with nose asunder and more than one knife scar. His hair was nicotine stained, and his clothes were rumpled, but clean. Something in his demeanor made me think he was drunk. With my paternal instincts at red alert, I stepped between him and my children and turned my back to him, putting up a wall of silence even as I used my body as a screen for my son and daughter.

He tried to speak once, but I didn't hear him clearly, and so I just nodded to acknowledge him. I sent the kids to a table across the room where I could keep an eye on them while I waited for our turn in line and where they wouldn't be near the man behind us.

"It's hard, isn't it?" he said. I glanced his way and nodded, mumbling something like "they grow up too fast," but scarcely made eye contact. He persisted, gently: "I mean it's hard raising them by yourself, isn't it?" Something in his tone made me turn to look at him. Only then did I notice his children, as I listened to him tell me how long his wife had been gone. His words contrasted with his hard exterior.

I was duly chastened. Once again I failed to see "my neighbor," as Jesus calls those people He places in our paths, in the way that Jesus might have seen him—despite the fact that Jesus never fails to see me with love, even through the scars of sin, even through the rumpled nature of my stutter-step faithfulness.

Today, Jesus walks with us into Starbucks, sits beside us on the commuter rail, and listens in during our meetings at work. He's as interested in us in these places as He is when we're pew-bound and singing praises. But He's also intrigued, compassionate, maybe even wistful about the people around us at Starbucks, on the train, or in the office. Many have never met Him, and few of us are moving slowly enough to think to introduce Him to them. While there is sadness in the eternal realm of these encounters, there must surely be a palpable disappointment He feels when we're so busy we fail to see the people in our paths the way He sees them, as sheep in need of a shepherd.

It is so very true that our work matters to God, but never more than people do.

May the pace of our lives never disrupt our ability to see our clients, our coworkers, and even our casual contacts with the same eyes that Jesus sees them. And may we always be open to moments when we can introduce them to Him.

WEEK 52

The Last Christmas Tale

Greater love has no one than this, that one lay down his life for his friends (JOHN 15:13).

IT'S CHRISTMAS EVE 1945, AND the tiny church is filled to capacity. Candles cast a soft glow in the dimly lit sanctuary. An elderly man steps to the pulpit and clears his throat slightly, gathering the attention of all in the room. "Our pastor asked me to read you this letter, written by his son last Christmas Eve."

The room grew absolutely still. Quietly, the deacon started reading:

Bastogne, Belgium
24 December, 1944

Dear Dad,

Your letter dated 22 November arrived a while ago. I'm saving it to open on Christmas. You cannot imagine what a gift it is to get mail here. Some guys who get no mail ask us to read ours out loud, just so they can hear from home, even if it isn't their home.

There are only six of us left now from the old gang. The rest are wounded, missing, or buried here on the other side of the world. The new guys seem so young, though most of them are only a year or two under us in age. They'll be old too, soon enough. It's so cold we can't stop shaking; our water freezes almost before we can drink it! Rockport seems so far away to me now. What I wouldn't give to be baking on its summer beaches again!

A stir near the rear of the auditorium caught the deacon's eye, causing him to pause and look up. Near the back of the room, an old man leaned on his cane as he struggled to his feet. Expecting him to leave the pew, a young couple stepped aside to let him out, but he merely nodded and stood in place. Another man one row back also stood. Then another, and another, until eventually every man in the congregation was on his feet. The reader at the pulpit turned to the pastor, who looked across the crowd, deeply moved by this show of respect for his son. The elder resumed his reading:

> *All those years you gave sermons on Christmas, I never really understood how a person could love somebody enough to give his life for them. But these guys, Dad! I know it must sound silly, but you don't live and fight with someone without growing to love them. I know there are bigger reasons why we fight wars, but for us here on the ground, it's about protecting each other, simple as that. For the first time in my life, I understand there's something worth dying for, and that's the guy in my foxhole. I've seen men scared beyond belief do amazing things when their buddies are in trouble.*
>
> *Tonight I heard singing across the fields where the Germans are camped. I didn't know the words, but the music was familiar. It's hard to believe the soldiers over there are singing "Silent Night" in their language, being the enemy and all. Still it makes me wonder if they aren't doing the same thing we are, fighting not for Hitler and his minions, but for their own buddies next to them. It almost makes me wish we could shake hands and just go home. But we can't, and we know it.*
>
> *No disrespect, Dad, but I'm not sure anyone can understand the story of Christmas better than the soldier. If he can give up a chance to see life through just because his friends are in trouble, then certainly God can love us that much. Surely that explains how Jesus could give up His place in heaven to come to earth.*

As the reader paused to draw a breath, only the sniffs and sounds of muffled crying broke the silence. He continued:

> *Not all of us are Christians here, Dad, and I'm sorry for that. Death comes so quickly to some that I just know they didn't have time to prepare to meet their Maker. I know it worries you that I'm here.*

When I signed up, I was so sure nothing could happen to me! Now what I want most is to be warm again; to be someplace quiet and safe. I want to get married, drive a new car, and all those things it feels like I'll never do now. I don't want to leave this world, nobody here does, but every day it looks more and more like most of us will. I want you to know, Dad, never before has Christmas meant so much to me. The story of the baby Jesus gives me hope in a place where there's very little reason to have hope.

I know if I don't make it, I'll be buried over here, and it makes me sad to think you won't even be able to visit my grave. But what joy we share knowing there will be a day when we all can see each other again in a place where we never will be sad or hurt or sorry again. So that's my Christmas present to you, Dad. Know that this Christmas, I understand better than ever before all those things you tried so hard to teach me. Give my love to Mom. I'll write again when I'm able.

Love,
Tommy

Not a dry eye could be found in the sanctuary that evening, one full year after the letter was written. The men in the sanctuary continued to stand out of respect for the pastor's son, and the ladies bowed their heads, showing their respect as they prayed quietly for the pastor and his family. The pastor continued to sit through this quiet salute, absorbing the love of his people for him and his son.

After a few moments, a man seated to his left stood and stepped to the podium to lead the congregation in carols. As he did, the congregation erupted in applause. Perhaps only on the first Christmas night did the appearance of a father's son cause more joy.

WEEK 53

Old Ideas for a New Year

Teach us to number our days aright, that we may gain a heart of wisdom (PSALM 90:12 NIV).

HERE ARE TEN NEW TESTAMENT Scriptures to help you in setting workplace goals, organizing your management strategies, and writing up your New Year's work/life resolutions.

1. *When the boss isn't looking:* Whatever you do, work at it with all your heart, as working for the Lord, not for men, since you know that you will receive an inheritance from the Lord as a reward. It is the Lord Christ you are serving (Colossians 3:23–24 NIV).

2. *About that temper tantrum or water cooler gossip:* If anyone considers himself religious and yet does not keep a tight rein on his tongue, he deceives himself and his religion is worthless (James 1:26 NIV).

3. *Management training that works:* Who is wise and understanding among you? Let him show it by his good life, by deeds done in the humility that comes from wisdom. But if you harbor bitter envy and selfish ambition in your hearts, do not boast about it or deny the truth. Such "wisdom" does not come down from heaven but is earthly, unspiritual, of the devil. For where you have envy and selfish ambition, there you find disorder and every evil practice. But the wisdom that comes from heaven is first of all pure; then peace-loving, considerate, submissive, full of mercy and good fruit, impartial and sincere. Peacemakers who sow in peace raise a harvest of righteousness (James 3:13–18 NIV).

4. *On looking the other way:* Anyone, then, who knows the good he ought to do and doesn't do it, sins (James 4:17 NIV).

5. *On not paying enough—or not paying at all—and even (sometimes) thinking, "Let's see how cheaply we can hire them":* Look! The wages you failed to pay the workmen who mowed your fields are crying out against you. The cries of the harvesters have reached the ears of the Lord Almighty (James 5:4 NIV).

6. *On anger and intimidation as management styles; on filling out performance evaluations; on talking about the boss behind his or her back:* Do not let any unwholesome talk come out of your mouths, but only what is helpful for building others up according to their needs, that it may benefit those who listen (Ephesians 4:29 NIV).

7. *On doing it because everyone else is or just because it's legal:* See to it that no one takes you captive through hollow and deceptive philosophy, which depends on human tradition and the basic principles of this world rather than on Christ (Colossians 2:8 NIV).

8. *On wages, working conditions, and management styles:* Masters, provide your slaves with what is right and fair, because you know that you also have a Master in heaven (Colossians 4:1 NIV).

9. *On career planning and assessment:* Make it your ambition to lead a quiet life, to mind your own business and to work with your hands, just as we told you, so that your daily life may win the respect of outsiders and so that you will not be dependent on anybody (1 Thessalonians 4:11–12).

10. *How much is enough?* But godliness with contentment is great gain. For we brought nothing into the world, and we can take nothing out of it. But if we have food and clothing, we will be content with that. People who want to get rich fall into temptation and a trap and into many foolish and harmful desires that plunge men into ruin and destruction. For the love of money is a root of all kinds of evil. Some people, eager for money, have wandered from the faith and pierced themselves with many griefs (1 Timothy 6:6–10).

Let this be the year people mark you as the go-to person for competence, integrity, and compassion; *but even more urgently,* let this be the year they mark you as the person they seek out first when their little girl needs prayer or they need hope or help.

Note to the Reader

THE PUBLISHER INVITES YOU TO share your response to the message of this book by writing Discovery House Publishers, Box 3566, Grand Rapids, MI 49501, USA. For information about other Discovery House books, music, or videos, contact us at the same address or call 1-800-653-8333. Find us on the Internet at http://www.dhp.org/ or send e-mail to books@dhp.org.